Mary Fields
(Black Mary)

Mary Fields at St. Peter's Mission, Montana, circa 1893.

Mary Fields

(Black Mary)

James A. Franks

WILD GOOSE PRESS
Santa Cruz, California

Copyright © 2000 by James A. Franks

All rights reserved. No part of this book may be reproduced or utilized in any form or by any means, electronic or mechanical, including photocopying, recording, or by any information storage or retrieval system, without permission in writing from the Publisher. Address inquiries to: Wild Goose Press, 719 Fairmount Avenue, Santa Cruz, California 95062 http://www.wildgoosepress.com

Most photographs used courtesy of St. Peter's Mission, Montana.

Library of Congress Control Number 00-136018

ISBN 0-9657173-4-8

Printed in the United States of America

First Edition

10 9 8 7 6 5 4 3 2 1

*O*ne of the most loved characters who lives in the memory of the Montana Ursulines was Mary Fields. The oldtimers called her "Black Mary" and they, too, loved and respected her. The Sisters provided for all of Mary's wants—board, clothing, spending money, cartridges, and tobacco. She was at times troublesome, but her unfailing loyalty endeared her to the Nuns and children.

—Sister Genevieve McBride, O.S.U.
The Bird Tail, 1974

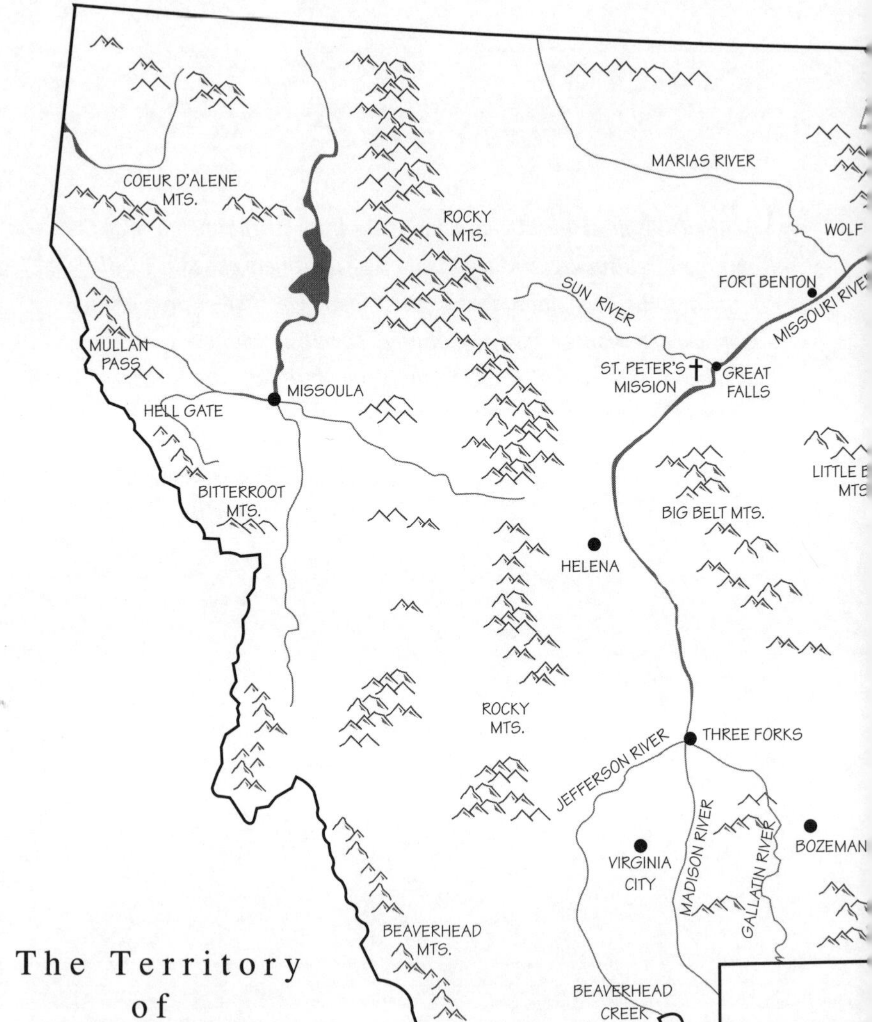

The Territory of MONTANA

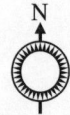

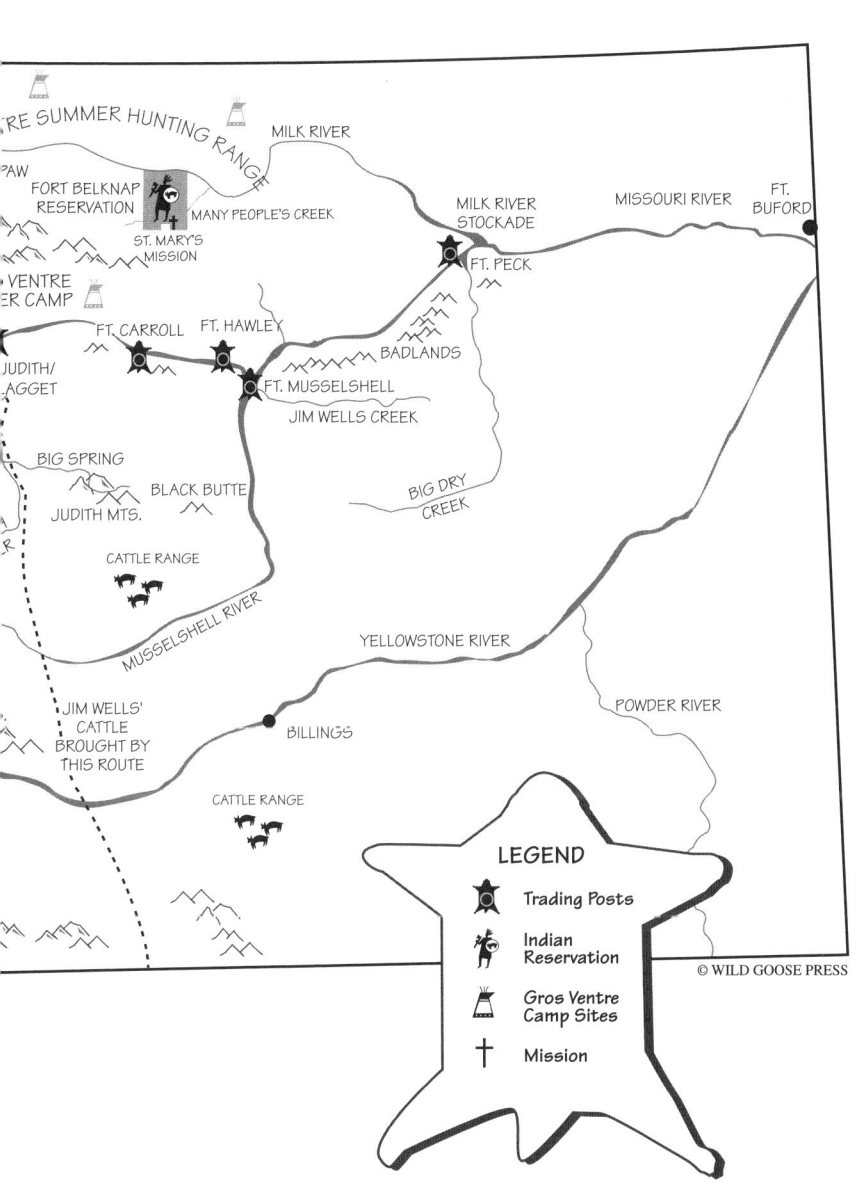

Contents

Preface	*xi*
Acknowledgments	*xiii*
Introduction	*1*
Chapter 1: *Tennessee*	*3*
Chapter 2: *Slavery in America*	*7*
Chapter 3: *The Birth of Mary Fields*	*11*
Chapter 4: *Growing Up on the Farm*	*15*
Chapter 5: *The "Black-White Nigger"*	*21*
Chapter 6: *The War*	*25*
Chapter 7: *Working for the Ursulines*	*29*
Chapter 8: *Early Missions in Montana*	*33*
Chapter 9: *Mary Heads West*	*37*
Chapter 10: *Mary Fields Meets Mary Wells*	*43*
Chapter 11: *The Wells Family*	*47*

CHAPTER 12: *From White to Indian*	53
CHAPTER 13: *Tragedy at the Mission*	65
CHAPTER 14: *Growing Pains*	71
CHAPTER 15: *Joseph Gump*	77
CHAPTER 16: *Mary Plays Matchmaker*	87
CHAPTER 17: *Festivals at the Mission*	95
CHAPTER 18: *Joseph Goes Courting*	101
CHAPTER 19: *Gunfight at the Mission*	109
CHAPTER 20: *Mary Says Good-bye*	113
CHAPTER 21: *The Wedding of Mary and Joseph*	123
CHAPTER 22: *Driving with the Bird*	127
CHAPTER 23: *A Trip to Tennessee*	135
CHAPTER 24: *A Baby in Marysville*	139
CHAPTER 25: *Visiting the Mission*	145
CHAPTER 26: *Mary's Last Years*	153
EPILOGUE	157
BIBLIOGRAPHY	159

Preface

As I did my research for my earlier books, *James Wells of Montana* and *Mary Wells*, a character important in Montana history and in my family history kept coming forward. I first heard about this character from my grandfather, Joseph Gump, who worked at St. Peter's Mission and married my grandmother there on July 23, 1895. This person, Mary Fields (Black Mary), was much loved by all.

She was a friend of my grandfather, a protector of my grandmother, and "God-sent" to Mother Amadeus and the sisters at St. Peter's Mission. I personally feel that her devotion to Mother Amadeus and the mission was never fully appreciated. I know her loyalty to Mother Amadeus could never be questioned, although I myself do not completely understand it.

Mary Fields is immortalized in Charlie Russell's pen-and-ink sketch, "A Quiet Day in Cascade." I hope this book will do her honor.

Acknowledgments

I AM GRATEFUL TO the Ursuline Convent at Great Falls, Montana, and to Sister Genevieve McBride, O.S.U., with whom I spent many hours.

I am grateful also to my grandparents, Joseph and Mary Gump; to Thermond Adams, my chief advisor on black history; and especially to Mary Fields (Black Mary) for being part of my grandparents' life.

Mary Fields
(Black Mary)

Introduction

WHAT WAS STORYTELLING for the blacks and Native Americans here in the New World called America? Was it a way to preserve their history? A way to pass on traditions, foods, and medicines? Storytelling was all of these, and a very important part of preserving history, since the whites tried hard to destroy both cultures.

In the same ways, the Indians and blacks would gather their families around the fire for an evening of storytelling. They would begin with uncannily similar stories of creation—how in the beginning there was no earth, only water. The only living things were two spirits who floated about listlessly in the company of a large ducklike bird. The spirits grew tired of all the water and wanted to make dry land for other creatures. They commanded the bird to dive down and bring up mud from the bottom.

The spirits pressed the mud into bricks and let it dry. Some they cast over the water, causing the land to materialize. They rolled the mud in their fingers and threw it into the New Earth to create man and woman. The spirits next made earthen images of all the creatures, blowing on them to bring them to life. The newly created men and women began to marry, have families, and become the people of the land. The greatest creature, to the Indians, was the buffalo; to the blacks it was the cattle.

This recital of tales served as both entertainment and instruction; it was also a form of worship and prayer. The tales would stress morals for the youth, who were always taught they could achieve greatness by their efforts.

Storytelling is important in understanding these two cultures, black and red, because it wasn't only the stories that were similar. Many of the traditions and herbs brought to America by the black slaves were similar to those of the Native Americans. If the whites could destroy the culture, they could destroy the will of the people. But the storytelling did survive, and storytelling is still very important in both cultures. It is done not only in words, sitting around a fire, but also by enactment in their dances and songs, or by the deeds of warriors in battle.

The youth are taught to observe all aspects of nature—such as which side of a tree has the lighter bark or the most moss on the branches. Their eyes are trained to penetrate the depths of darkness. Animals, no matter how small, were respected because they showed the people how to gather food, how to survive. It is a mystery how people from such far distant places could hold so many stories and practices in common.

This is a story about a great black woman from Tennessee who became a protector to a half-breed Montana Indian. In her life, these two great cultures coalesced. It is the story of Mary Fields, known as Black Mary, as it was told to me by my grandfather. The story will include some historical background of Tennessee, which is important in showing how the Indians were driven out and the black slaves brought into the area.

CHAPTER ONE

Tennessee

MARY FIELDS WAS BORN in Hickman County, Tennessee, in 1832. She was born a slave on a farm owned by the Dunne family. Hickman County is in Middle Tennessee, southwest of Nashville, in an area with large farms. The term "farm" was used in Tennessee rather than "plantation." The farms required fewer slaves to plant and harvest their tobacco, corn, and cotton crops than did the big plantations.

Tennessee, like most of the New World, was originally populated by Native Americans (Indians) known as Moundbuilders. They had been in this area for over a thousand years. The Cherokee Indians claimed Middle Tennessee as their hunting ground. The Chickamauga Indians lived near the present site of Chattanooga, while the Chickasaw occupied West Tennessee.

In 1540 a party of Spanish explorers led by Hernando de Soto raided some of the Indian villages in the valley of the Tennessee River, killing many of the Indians for little or no reason. Moving westward, de Soto became the first European to reach the Mississippi River, which he came upon in 1541. He then left the Tennessee region. No other explorers entered the area until 1673, when James Needham and Gabriel Arthur of England explored the Tennessee River Valley. At least they didn't kill any Indians, as de Soto had.

That same year, Louis Joliet of Canada and Father Jacques Marquette of France sailed down the Mississippi. In 1682, Robert Cavalier, Sieur de La Salle, claimed the entire Mississippi Valley for France and built Fort Prudhomme on the Chickasaw Bluffs. But the post was so isolated that the French soon had to abandon it. French settlers began moving into the Mississippi Valley, which they called New France. In 1714, Charles Charleville set up a French trading post at French Lick.

France, Spain, and England all claimed the Tennessee region. All three countries competed for the trade and friendship of the Indians. The dispute eventually became a contest between the British and the French. The French and Indian War broke out between British and French settlers in 1754. The British outnumbered the French by about twenty to one, but the French won decisive victories during the early years of the war. After nine bloody years, the British won out. In 1763, by the Treaty of Paris, the French surrendered to the British all claims to the lands east of the Mississippi.

By 1769, permanent settlers lived in the Tennessee region. New white settlers began to come into the area from Virginia and North Carolina. The Tennessee region belonged to the British colony of North Carolina, but vast, rugged mountains separated the settlers in Tennessee from the protection of the mother colony. In 1772 a group of settlers established law and order, as they called it, in the wilderness by forming their own government, the Watauga Association. They drew up one of the first written constitutions in North America.

A group called the Transylvania Company bought a large area of Tennessee and Kentucky from the Cherokee in 1775. Daniel Boone, working for the company, blazed a trail from Virginia across the mountains at Cumberland Gap to open this land to settlement. Boone's trail, the famous Wilderness Road, became the main route to settlement.

In 1779 two groups of pioneers, led by James Robertson and John Donelson, pushed far into the wilds and settled around the Big Salt Lick on the Cumberland River. They built Fort Nashborough, which formed the center of the Middle Tennessee settlements. These pioneers drew up an agreement called the Cumberland Compact. It established representative government for all settlers and created a court system to enforce its provisions.

In 1780, during the Revolutionary War, John Sevier led a group of pioneers from the Tennessee region across the Great Smoky Mountains into South Carolina. These men helped American forces win a victory over the British at the battle of King's Mountain on October 2.

Meanwhile, the settlers and Indians were trying to drive each other out of the Tennessee region. The Indians had been there thousands of years; the whites had been there for less than two hundred years, and in most of this region for only five years. The settlers appealed for help to North Carolina, but the help did not come. In 1784, three counties in East Tennessee revolted against North Carolina and formed the independent state of Franklin. They made John Sevier, the hero of King's Mountain, their governor.

North Carolina regained control of the area in 1788, then, in 1789, gave the Tennessee region to the United States. The federal government made it into a new territory, called the Territory of the United States South of the River Ohio. William Blount became the first and only governor of this territory.

On February 6, 1796, Tennessee adopted a constitution in preparation for statehood. It became the sixteenth state in the Union (and the first state to be created out of government territory) on June 1, 1796. Tennessee elected John Sevier as its first governor. The new state had a population of about 77,000 whites, with no Indians and only a few Negroes counted.

In 256 years, the Native Americans were pushed from their territory and the whites had a new population to do their work: the Negroes. Negro slaves were used on the West and Middle Tennessee farms, while the farmers in the eastern part of the state did not own slaves. The free Negroes could vote and were counted in the Tennessee population until a new constitution was adopted in 1834, which took the franchise away from them. This is the condition into which Mary Fields was born.

Chapter Two

Slavery in America

Between 1600 and 1850, Western Europe and America grew strong and wealthy. They were making great scientific and manufacturing advances and were becoming centers of world power. When this period began, there was a grave difference of power between Europe and Africa. The Europeans were further ahead in technical knowledge, and were entering the age of modern science and machinery.

American recorded history started with an Italian sailor named Christopher Columbus. The King and Queen of Spain offered to pay for his trip across the unknown Atlantic Ocean. Columbus hoped to be able to sail across the Atlantic and find a shorter route to China and India. He found instead the islands of the Caribbean Sea. Not realizing how far he was from India, Columbus named these islands the West Indies. So the people became known as "Indians."

Many ships sailed after Columbus; within a few years the soldiers of Spain had reached Central America and found the Pacific Ocean. The Spanish military in the West Indies and Central America grabbed all the riches they could get their hands on. They burned, ruined, and destroyed the existing population and started cultivating the land. But the land needed workers and the Spanish would not work in the fields, so they forced the Indians to work for them. These people were turned into slaves, and large numbers of them died in their bonds.

The Spanish looked for more workers. First they tried to find them in Europe, but they couldn't get enough. Then Spain saw that the Portuguese were bringing captives from Africa. What was a small business would become a huge trade. Africa was becoming trapped in a fate from which there would be no escape for more than three hundred years.

Following the Spanish and the Portuguese, the English sailed into the Caribbean and settled on some of the islands. The French followed, then the Dutch. At the same time the French and English began to fight each other for the rich farmlands of the coast of mainland North America.

These American and Caribbean lands were excellent for growing two crops: sugar and tobacco. Both were in demand throughout Europe. These crops required millions of plantation workers, who were found in Africa and captured to become slaves. Thus Mary Fields' ancestors, among many others, were brought to America.

This was called the Great Circuit trade. Europeans bought cheap goods at home, such as cotton cloth and hardware, which were then sent to Africa. These goods were sold to African chiefs in exchange for human captives, who were shipped across the Atlantic and sold as slaves. Then the same captains bought sugar and tobacco and took these crops back to Europe, where they sold for high prices. This route would be repeated over and over: Europe to Africa to America, and back again.

The European countries made their separate profits. The factory owners made a profit when they sold their cheap goods to the ship owners. The ship owners made a profit when they sold African captives for sugar and tobacco. Then they made a second profit when they sold their sugar and tobacco in Europe.

In 1719 England was shipping 18,771 tons of goods per year. By 1792 this had risen to 260,322 tons. All this was built on the slave trade.

In wide sections of African seacoast, the kings, chiefs, and businessmen had got themselves trapped into the business of collecting and selling captives. The western coast of Africa became little more than a place from which to export slaves. This caused destruction in many countries of Africa from which they have not recovered even to the present day.

The African kings and chiefs, having got themselves into the slave trade, could not get out. They had no way of knowing that the slave trade would become Europe's biggest interest in Africa. Raiding for captives caused wars between African states. The chiefs who had the most firearms won the war. The need for more firearms led to the chase for more captives, and the need for more captives led in turn to the need for more firearms, which were made in Europe. Europe would trade them for slaves.

This destruction of Africa started to come to an end in 1807, when England lost interest in the plantation in the New World. The English began to speak out against the idea of making slaves of Africans. The French soon stopped practicing slavery, but not the Portuguese or the Americans. They went right on capturing and using slaves until the mid-1800s.

Chapter Three

The Birth of Mary Fields

THE DUNNE FAMILY had come from Ireland. They had money and were able to purchase a large tract of land in Hickman County. With the purchase of a few slaves from the North Carolina slave markets, they were able to make their farm profitable.

By 1832, the Dunne farm had forty-five slaves. This included a staff of house slaves, one of whom was a woman called Suzanna. Suzanna became pregnant by a field hand who was known as Buck. The Dunnes allowed Suzanna to live down in the slave quarters with Buck as if married, but as soon as her baby was born in 1832, Buck was sold off. The Dunnes did not want their house Negro to have more children.

The selling of her mate almost killed Suzanna. He was good to her and she loved him. He was sent to a North Carolina slave market to be sold so there would be no trace of where he ended up. This was a very common practice to ensure that slaves who tried to run off would not be able to find their family members.

Suzanna could hear those haunting words: "Now, gentlemen and fellow citizens, here is a big, black buck Negro." *Her* big, black buck Negro. "He's stout as a mule. Good for any kind of work and he never gives any trouble. How much am I offered for him?" Suzanna would say to herself, "I give the world for him, but he is gone."

The possibility of being sold away from family and friends had always caused constant apprehension and worry among the slaves. Suzanna had never thought that such a fateful moment would come to her. She pleaded with her master not to separate her from her husband, but her pleas were ignored and he was chained for his arduous journey.

Suzanna's daughter was called Mary. Mary's mother didn't have a last name, and Mary's father was just Buck, a name given to many of the male slaves. But Suzanna felt her daughter must have a last name like the whites. Since her father was a man of the fields, a field slave, she called her Mary Fields. From the day of her birth, Suzanna made the strong point to all that her daughter would be known as Mary Fields, not just Mary.

Before she had fully recovered from the shock of having her mate sold off, Suzanna was told by her mistress that she would be moving to the room behind the kitchen of the big house. She must stop nursing her own daughter, Mary, so she could nurse the mistress's daughter, Dolly, who had been born within two weeks of Mary's birth. Mary could go on cow's or goat's milk, or Suzanna could find another slave woman who had just given birth to nurse her. But Suzanna continued to nurse her baby in secret, with the help of another house slave. She kept up her hope that she would produce enough milk for both children.

Suzanna wanted to raise Mary as a house slave, or "house nigger" as they were called. She had seen many children taken from the house and put back in the slave quarters to be raised by one of the women who were too old to work in the fields. But to Suzanna's surprise, from the very first it seemed that Mrs. Dunne was happy to have the two babies together in the house. This pleased Suzanna; she could have Mary with her while she watched Dolly. Suzanna became a personal maid to Mrs. Dunne and Dolly. This new role made life much easier for her.

The two children grew quickly and were healthy. Mrs. Dunne was good to Suzanna and Mary; she made sure Mary always had good clothes, and sometimes would have Suzanna dress the girls alike. When the girls played in the yard, many smiled to see one child so white and one so black who were friends. It was clear to the other slaves that Mrs. Dunne showed favor to Suzanna and Mary and was happy to have them around, providing a friend for her only daughter.

CHAPTER FOUR

Growing Up on the Farm

THE DUNNE FARM BECAME MORE BEAUTIFUL and productive with each passing year. It showed all the work and pride put into it. The slaves had plenty of food, warm clothes, and comfortable, though very simple, housing called "the quarters." The master's house was called the "great house."

Suzanna learned one of the reasons the Dunnes were better to their slaves than most was that they were Catholic. The Catholic Church had come out against slavery, although it was not doing much to stop the practice. So the Dunnes felt that if they treated their slaves a little better they would be justified in owning them.

The Dunnes never tried to convert their slaves and never interfered with their African practices. The Dunne farm was considered special because one of the slave women was a healer who put up medicines and used leeches to bleed people for healing.

When Suzanna was hanging clothes one day, she was bitten by a snake. Mrs. Dunne made a poultice of warm ashes and vinegar. The old healer stripped a dozen agave plants in vinegar and applied the cantala vinegar to the inflamed leg. The leg healed. She said the Indians were accustomed to apply wet ashes, or plunge the limb into strong lye.

The old woman had no other name but "the old healer." She told Suzanna, "I tell you and I show you, Suzanna, how to smell a snake. You smell that snake, you make him go one way, you go the other, then you no get bit."

The old healer was respected and called upon for her knowledge by the slaves from all the farms around. The Dunnes would allow her to visit the sick and deliver medicines and herbs without any restrictions.

As MARY GREW SHE DIDN'T FEEL LIKE A SLAVE, since much of her time was spent with Dolly Dunne; whatever Dolly was taught, Mary would learn. She could see the hard life of the slaves and her mother made sure she had contact with them, but she was Dolly's slave and friend. Mrs. Dunne would have Mary fan flies when she sat on the porch and perform other little tasks, so Mary always knew her place. But the Dunne family made sure that she was treated well, and she was actually allowed to eat at the dinner table with the family.

Suzanna worried that if the children ever had a falling-out, Mary wouldn't know her role as a slave. So she made sure Mary went to the slaves' church on Sundays. The white folks would go in the morning and the slaves would go after dinner. The slaves' church was made out of hand-sawed planks and put together with homemade nails. But it was the slaves' place to praise God.

By the time they were ten, Mary did everything with Dolly—they would ride together, play together, and eat together. Dolly never seemed to see how black Mary was; they were friends.

Suzanna continued to worry about Mary's closeness to the whites. She still hated them for separating her from her husband, and they could do the same to her and Mary at any time. She also worried about Mary as she grew up. She didn't want her to become a white man's personal property and have what they called "old-yellow nigger" babies. Suzanna would tell Mary over and over, "Mary, you must remember you isn't his'n." As Mary started to mature, Suzanna would force her to eat more. She felt if she fed the girl more she would become fat and not be attractive to the white men; she felt sure Mary could handle any of the black men.

By the age of twelve Mary seemed to have reached her full height, not more than five feet two inches, and she was chubby. Mary also started to menstruate that year, and Suzanna had to show her how to take care of herself the slave way. The whites used menstrual rags that the slaves had to wash. But the slaves would take a gourd, cut it in half, take the inside out and dry it. The gourd shells were used for drinking cups, while the dried inside of the gourd was put in a cloth and used to absorb the menstrual flow. This African method worked much better than the rags, but the whites thought it primitive and would laugh at the slaves for doing it.

Mary was given chores by Mrs. Dunne and Suzanna that she did with ease. And she was always right back at Dolly's side. The Dunne family felt Mary was good for Dolly, giving her a friend on the farm.

WHEN MARY TURNED FOURTEEN, her world changed. Her mother died. All the healers and white doctors the Dunnes brought in couldn't help. Suzanna just started to get weak, and within two months she was dead.

Her body was taken down to the slave quarters and Mary was told to stay with her as her body was washed, dressed in her best dress, and put into a small wooden casket. The old healer blessed her body by blowing smoke from her pipe into Suzanna's mouth, eyes, nose, and ears as she said special prayers. Many of the prayers that were said Mary couldn't understand, since the healer spoke a language she had never heard before; it was a tribal language.

Suzanna was buried in the slave cemetery in a simple box built by the black carpenter out of scrap wood found around the farm. The whole Dunne family was there and provided some beautiful flowers. Dolly hugged Mary all during the burial. The friends cried together. The only family Mary had now was the Dunnes.

That night was the first time in Mary's life she had been completely alone in that room behind the kitchen. She cried herself to sleep.

The next day she was called in by Mrs. Dunne, who told her she would stay in the big house but would take over her mother's duties. Mary spent the day taking the few things her mother had down to the slave quarters to give to those in need. It was the first time in a long time that Mary wondered where her father was and where her mother had come from.

With her new duties Mary was required to wear the dress of a servant; her hair must be cut off and she would wear a rag on her head. But it wasn't long before Mary found she could do all her chores and still have plenty of time to be with Dolly.

MARY WASN'T SUPPOSED TO KNOW about Mr. Dunne having a colored woman. Once in a while he would drink a little whiskey and sneak down to the slave quarters. In later years Mary would say, "We all knew plenty of colored women have children by white men. They take them children what have their own blood and make slaves out of them. If the missus found out she might kill them. But she hardly ever found out, 'cause no one ever talks. The white men not given to tell and the nigger women always afraid to. My mother said she hoping that things won't be that way always." Mary was sure Mr. Dunne had one yellow baby.

CHAPTER FIVE

The "Black-White Nigger"

WHEN BOTH MARY AND DOLLY turned sixteen years old, Dolly was to be sent off to Toledo, Ohio, to a boarding school run by the Ursuline order. This was again hard for Mary, since her only friend was now leaving. The big house became a lonesome place for Mary; her mother had died a couple of years earlier, and the Dunnes were becoming very old.

Mary found herself spending more time down with the slaves. Some of the first things she learned were how to smoke and how to drink the homemade liquor, which could be made from anything—corn, potatoes, or rye. Mary was interested in learning the ways of the slaves and she would take part in all their ceremonies and traditions. She wanted to learn all that her mother had kept away from her. Since Mary could read and write, she was able to make notes on everything. She was also learning an African language of the slaves.

She started her own garden and hennery so she could sell eggs and make extra money. The slaves would make fun of her, calling her the "black-white nigger." But nothing would stop her from learning; she wanted to learn about herbs, medicine, and religion. One of the first songs she learned and would catch herself singing was this:

> My knee bones achin',
> My body is 'rackin' with pain.
> I calls myself de child of God,
> Heaven am my aim.
> If you don't believe I'se a child of God,
> Just meet me on de other shore.
> Heaven is my home,
> I calls myself a child of God.
> I'se a long time on my way,
> But heaven am my home.

When Dolly came home for the summers she would spend less time on the farm and less time with Mary. She had a new world and life and Mary was less a part of it. When Dolly finished high school, she stayed in Ohio and started college.

The more Dolly was away, the harder it was on Mary. As she became older, she was becoming more of a slave than part of the Dunne family. Still, she continued to be treated better than most of the slaves because she remained in the big house and not in the slaves' quarters.

By the time Mary was twenty years old she weighed over two hundred pounds and was a very strong person who could handle herself in any situation. Mary's garden was always the best on the farm and she kept expanding her hennery. She continually tried new plants to find out what grew best. She had also become a carpenter, building her own new hen house. Mary was becoming an advisor to the slaves.

As time passed, Dolly came home less often; she spent one summer in Europe, another on the East Coast. But whenever

Dolly did come home, Mary was always there to help her friend. Again Dolly would spend time at the other farms at parties and dances.

In 1854, when Mary and Dolly would both be twenty-two years old, Mr. Dunne called Mary into his study to tell her that Dolly was entering the convent to become an Ursuline nun. She would not be returning to the farm for the next five years.

This was hard on Mary; she had lost her best and only friend, as she thought, forever. She didn't know what it meant to join a convent, and it took her a while to get the courage to ask Mr. Dunne to explain it. When she did ask, the explanation was hard to understand. Dolly would join a group of women who couldn't marry and would dedicate their lives to God. Their life's work would be to help others. Dolly would take a new name, the name of a saint. Mary still didn't understand any of this, but it felt good being able to talk to Mr. Dunne about the new life Dolly had chosen.

In the spring of 1856, Mrs. Dunne died. She wasn't sick; one night she just died. To Mary's surprise, the Order did not allow Dolly to come home for her mother's funeral. It must have been hard on Dolly; it was very hard on Mr. Dunne not having her home.

People from all the farms around came to the funeral, and Mary and the other house slaves helped make food for all of them. Mrs. Dunne was buried on the farm in a special area with a small white wooden fence around it.

With Mrs. Dunne's death, Mr. Dunne seemed to lose interest in the farm; with only Mr. Dunne to take care of, Mary found herself giving orders to the other servants. Dolly's brother, James, who had been to law school and was a lawyer in the town near the farm, would come out to give advice and help, but his interest was not the farm.

CHAPTER SIX

The War

Mary would hear Mr. Dunne and his son talking about the Confederate States of America being formed. The first Southern states to secede from the Union were South Carolina, Georgia, Louisiana, Mississippi, Florida, Alabama, and Texas. A provisional government was being set up in Montgomery, Alabama. The Dunnes felt that a war was coming, but were sure it would be a quick war that would be won by the South.

Then on April 12, 1861, P. T. Beauregard ordered the Confederate soldiers to fire on Fort Sumter and the open war began. With the firing on Fort Sumter, four more states joined the Confederacy: Arkansas, North Carolina, Virginia, and Tennessee. The Dunne farm was now in the Confederacy.

Mr. Dunne tried to explain to Mary what was going on. Despite the insistence of the abolitionists, President Lincoln did not immediately issue an edict freeing the slaves, lest it alienate the loyal border states. But on July 22, 1862, he read a draft to his cabinet, which was published all over the South. Only after a successful campaign did he issue a parliamentary edict, and then on January 1, 1863, the formal Emancipation Proclamation. This proclamation did not free all slaves in the United States, but only those in the rebel states.

The Dunne farm suffered from the very beginning. Mr. Dunne's son was made an officer in the Confederate Army and was thus unable to help on the farm. All the white overseers were taken off to war. Only old Mr. Dunne was left to run the farm.

Tennessee saw some of the biggest battles of the war. From the very first Tennessee was in the middle. First the Confederate Army took almost everything: grain, cattle, horses, and even Mary's chickens. What the South didn't take, the North did. The beautiful farm that Mary had spent her life on was now totally destroyed.

Mr. Dunne died in 1864, leaving Mary and a few slaves on the farm to take care of themselves. Mary took Mr. Dunne's shotgun and began to shoot wild game to feed the few slaves left. It hurt her to see the old slaves in the smokehouse scraping fat from the walls and the floor to use for flavor in their cooking. Many times Mary would go to the place where she had hidden a few seeds to start her garden again, wanting to eat them. But the old slaves showed her how to gather roots and wild vegetables. They were surviving.

The Confederacy fell apart after Lee's surrender on April 9, 1865. The Confederate states were readmitted to the Union and slavery was abolished. Mary was a free person, thirty-three years old, with no place to go.

Mary went to the other freed slaves who remained on the farm; many were old. She talked to them about staying and working the land. Mary was to be acting foreman since she could read and write. She rebuilt her hennery, kept her own garden, and stayed in the big house. But her role as foreman for the freed slaves kept expanding. As sharecroppers they had to find markets for their crop. This meant Mary had to bargain for them, sign contracts, help buy and sell animals. Being in the big house had been a good teacher for her. Mary also became the healer, using knowledge she had learned from the old healer before she died. But with all the hard work the ex-slaves put into the farm, it wasn't coming back, and the ex-slaves were poor.

Two years after the end of the war, James Dunne returned to the farm, having been held prisoner in the North. He told the ex-slaves the farm was being sold for taxes. Mary was offered a job as servant for the James Dunne family. She took the position; this would be the first time she had lived away from the farm since her birth. Since she was a free servant, she would receive room and board plus twenty dollars a month salary. She was treated well by the family and was happy, but she missed the other ex-slaves.

Mary still had her habits of smoking and drinking alcohol, which the Dunnes accepted. She was proud of herself because she had some money from the sale of her hens and chickens, and now was saving her salary.

CHAPTER SEVEN

Working for the Ursulines

I$_N$ 1878 DOLLY DUNNE, now Mother Amadeus, asked Mary to come to Toledo, Ohio, to work for the Ursuline convent and the girls' school they operated. Mary was now forty-six years old and ready to move to a new life; she was eager to be near her old friend.

A ticket was sent to her, and she packed her few possessions and left Tennessee for the first time. The trip would take twenty days. During the whole trip she was the only black person in the coach. When the coach stopped at night, Mary had to sleep in the coach or with the help, and her food was sent out to her. As they went further north, the situation improved. She was allowed to eat in the taverns, but still couldn't sleep in the guest rooms.

She did find herself playing cards at night in the taverns; here she made friends and was allowed to smoke and drink. She had learned to play cards from the slaves, who knew every trick. Mary became an amusement—this short, fat, cigar-smoking woman who could hold her own with cards and liquor. She was making money with cards on this trip.

A very young nun, Sister Sacred Heart Meilink, met the stage in Toledo. Mary and the sister got into a wagon for the short ride to the convent. This was a big three-story building that housed the nuns, the girls' school, and a dormitory. Mary was taken to her room, which had a big bed, a chest of drawers with a mirror over it, a nightstand, and a rocking chair. Then she was shown the bathroom and told she could clean up before meeting Mother Amadeus.

A short time later Sister Sacred Heart came to get Mary and take her to Mother Amadeus's office. Mother Amadeus greeted Mary with a big hug. The two sat talking a long time about the past and what Mary would be doing at the school. She would be supervising all the help, making sure the school and convent ran smoothly.

Mother Amadeus asked Mary if there was anything she needed. Mary answered, "Yes, a good cigar and a drink."

Mother Amadeus looked at Mary very seriously, trying to act stern, and then she started to laugh. She hugged her and said, "That is something you will have to handle on your own, and I know you will."

That evening at dinner, Mary sat at the head table with the sisters, to whom she was introduced. How was she going to remember all those long names—Sister Sacred Heart Meilink, Sister Saint Ignatius McFarland, Sister Francis Seibert, and on and on. It was so nice to be just Mary.

The girls from the boarding school sat at tables in front of the sisters' table. Mother Amadeus rang a small bell and there was total silence. Then a small girl stood and said, "Let us pray," and all heads bowed.

Bless us, O Lord, and these Thy gifts which we are about to receive from Thy bounty, through Christ our Lord. Amen.

When the little girl sat down, other girls came out with the food. The sisters were served first, along with Mary. It was a meat pie that was very bland, and the bread was dry. Mary said to herself, "This will change." The girls ate in complete silence. When everyone was finished Mother Amadeus rang her bell again and another little girl stood with another prayer:

> We give Thee thanks, Almighty God, for all Thy benefits, who livest and reignest world without end. Amen.

Then all the girls stood and filed out of the room, followed by the sisters. Mary could see some little girls coming in to clean up.

"Mother Amadeus," Mary asked, "who are these little girls doing the cleaning up?"

"Those girls pay their tuition through their work."

Mary went to her room and slept soundly that night. She first awoke to a small bell and could hear the sisters moving around. Mary had no idea of the time. She was told that breakfast would be at seven A.M., so she got up at six-thirty and was ready to go to the dining room at seven. The seating and prayers were the same as at dinner. They were served corn meal mush with bread, jam, and milk.

After breakfast Mother Amadeus took Mary around to see everything in the building and meet the help. Mary was surprised at how small the sisters' rooms were. The rooms, which were called cells, each had a small hard bed, a small desk, a lamp, and a cross on the wall. The rooms were half the size of the one Mary had been given.

Mary was anxious to start work. The first thing she did was to work with the cooks. She said, "We gotta make the food taste better," and she did.

Mary started a garden, built a hen house, and got a couple of pigs. She would say, "What people don't eat, pigs and chickens eat; then we eat them."

It was a surprise to the sisters how much Mary could do, and she never seemed tired. She did laundry, bought supplies, made sure meals were prepared, and did all the repairs on the convent, and she still had time for her beautiful vegetable garden and hennery. Mary kept an area in her room to dry her seeds for the next year's garden and her herbs for healing.

The sisters would ignore it when Mary slipped out to her hennery for a drink of liquor or a cigar or pipe. She told Mother Amadeus she would use only Tennessee tobacco that was sent to her by a friend in Tennessee.

Mary gained the love of everyone at the convent, from the workers to the sisters and students. Many times Mother Amadeus would look out the window and see Mary in her garden talking to one of the students. Mother Amadeus told the other sisters, "Mary was God-sent. She can solve any problem, and the children love her."

CHAPTER EIGHT

Early Missions in Montana

WHILE MARY WAS WORKING for the Ursuline nuns in Ohio, many things were happening in Montana that would change her life.

In 1859, the first mission among the Blackfoot Indians was established on the Teton River. It consisted of three squatters'-type log cabins put up quickly to provide winter quarters for the two Jesuit priests so they could study the Blackfoot language.

Father Adrian Hoelken, who built the place with the aid of Brother Vincent Magri, decided to move the mission site after only two months. (It was not uncommon for a mission to move several times before a suitable place was found.) The mission was moved to the Sun River. Again two cabins were built, but the Indians ran the missionaries off in less than five months.

In 1861, four Jesuits were again in Blackfoot country. Their superior was Father Giorda. Father Giorda and his Jesuits spent the winter at Fort Benton, looking for a site for the new mission.

In the spring they found a site on the Missouri River, and took possession on February 12, 1862. They dedicated the mission to St. Peter the Apostle.

The group consisted of Fathers Menetrey and Camillus Imoda, Brothers Francis DeKock and Lucian D'Agostino, and Father Giorda. The Indians, especially the Northern Blackfoot who were coming down from Canada, were still hostile. Father Giorda wondered how long St. Peter's on the Missouri would last.

A few days after he arrived, Father Giorda was walking on the ice of the Missouri River and fell through. He stretched out his arms and so sank only to his armpits. When he shouted for help, the two monks heard him, and so did an Indian who had pitched his tepee near the mission. The brothers tried to reach him, but the ice started to break. The Indian took his lariat, skillfully cast it around Father Giorda, and dragged him to safety.

Father Giorda stated that after God, he owed his life to this Blackfoot Indian. He made a solemn vow to devote the rest of his life to the salvation of the Blackfoot Indians.

St. Peter's was beset by raiding Indian war parties and struggled for the next three years. The mission cabins were dark and smoky, ill furnished, with bare earthen floors, little food, and no medicine. The missionaries had no cloth; they wore buckskin underclothing, trousers, and shirts under their cassocks. The buckskin clothes became a great home for lice. To try to kill the lice, the missionaries would put their clothes outside to freeze them, but starving wolves would eat the skin. When the missionaries were given conventional clothes, the Indians would steal them.

In 1865 gold brought many miners to the Sun River area, causing greater hatred of the Indians towards whites. This caused Father Giorda to move his mission to a site in the Little Belt Mountains, near the Indian landmark called Bird Tail Rock.

On December 5, 1870, President Grant announced a new peace policy in the administration of the reservations. The Blackfoot reservation was given over to the Methodists and the Jesuits were excluded from any work with the Blackfoot Indians. Then on April 15, 1874, without the approval of the Indians or the knowledge of the Jesuits, the boundaries of the Blackfoot reservation were rearranged, with its southern boundary sixty miles north of St. Peter's.

If the Jesuits had known this would happen, they would not have opened a mission at Bird Tail Rock. However, since they were already there when this injustice towards the Blackfoot occurred, they were determined to stay. The Jesuits converted the mission into a school.

Father Giorda died on August 4, 1882, and Father Damiani was appointed superior. The first lay teacher Father Damiani hired was the famous Canadian Métis leader Louis Riel, who had come to Montana to hide. A born revolutionary, the devoted and fiery Riel caused the father much concern with all his wild talk about Canadian politics and his heretical views on religion. Riel had come from the Red River Colony, which lay in the heart of the Northwest Fur Company's area of operations in Canada.

As the colony expanded, it interfered with the fur trade. The company became increasingly hostile. Company trappers in the region were Métis (people of mixed white and Indian ancestry). The Northwest Fur Company turned them against the settlers. The Métis tried to force the farmers to leave by burning their homes and destroying their crops. The violence reached a climax in 1816, when the Métis massacred the colonial governor and twenty men in the battle of Seven Oaks.

The Dominion of Canada was created in 1867, and Great Britain began the process of uniting the vast regions of Canada. The Métis of the Red River Valley opposed the union and rebelled. The Métis held no legal title to their lands, and feared they would lose the lands to the British Canadian settlers who would pour in once the union with Canada was finalized.

Louis Riel used buffalo hunters as soldiers. They turned back the settlers, captured Fort Garry, and set up their own government. Then the Canadian government took over the area by force and Louis Riel fled to Montana. Only the Jesuits would dare to hire such a dangerous man.

Riel left St. Peter's in 1884 to lead the Riel Rebellion in Saskatchewan. He was captured, tried for treason, and hanged. Riel had been a good teacher who would long be remembered by the schoolboys at St. Peter's Mission School.

FATHER DAMIANI WOULD SAY that a mission school without sisters was no mission school at all. He pressed hard to obtain Ursulines for the girls' school at St. Peter's. They arrived shortly after Louis Riel left, and it was Mother Amadeus who led them.

CHAPTER NINE

Mary Heads West

MOTHER AMADEUS TOLD MARY that she had been meeting with Father Damiani. He wanted the Ursuline nuns to go out to St. Peter's Mission to start a girl's school, and she would lead the Ursulines to Montana. This was a shock to Mary, who was happy working at the convent and being near her old friend.

Mother Amadeus tried to explain to Mary that she had given her life to God, and if God wanted her to go to the Montana missions, she must go. Mary asked Mother Amadeus if she could go with her to Montana, but Mother Amadeus said the request was for four Ursulines only, since the housing was very limited and primitive.

Mary worked closely with the Ursulines helping them prepare for their trip west. Along with books and supplies for the school, they packed medicines and special herbs, which Mary marked with instructions for their use.

The time came for Mother Amadeus to leave, with three other sisters, in late September 1884. Mary prepared a special dinner for her friend. When the nuns left, she could feel tears in her eyes as she said good-bye again to her friend. Mary stayed busy with her work, but waited for the letters to come back from Montana; they were always given to her to read.

The letters told of the sisters arriving at the mission on a very cold October day. They would be required to establish their convent and school in a couple of log cabins. Mother Amadeus wrote that they had thirty little Indian girls to accommodate in this small space.

In January 1885, Mother Amadeus became sick with pneumonia and wrote to ask Mary Fields to come to Montana. When Mary read the letter, she didn't even have to think about it. Within a couple of days she had packed her things, which included a few hens, a rooster, her herbs, and many special seeds for a garden. A ticket was purchased for her; she said her many goodbyes to all her friends at the convent and school, and the sisters took her to the stage line.

On the trip to Helena, Montana, she made sure at every stop that her chickens were fed and cared for. The trip was long and hard, but Mary was happy to be going to Montana.

From Helena she was taken by wagon to St. Peter's Mission School. During the trip Mary had become a novelty to all—this short, fat, very black woman, going to Montana with her crate of chickens. She was an even greater surprise when she would pull out one of her hand-rolled cigars or her pipe and light them up, sitting back with her eyes closed, enjoying every puff.

Mary Fields was fifty-three years old and starting a new life in Montana.

BEFORE THE WAGON HAD EVEN STOPPED, Mary was heading for the cabin where Mother Amadeus lay. As soon as the nun had Mary at her side, she started to recover. She knew Mary had real healing powers. Mary made a medicine from lobelia; she used the leaves and stems, boiling them in water and making her patient drink it a little at a time. Then she would roast onions until soft, extract the liquid, add honey, mix it well, and give this to Mother Amadeus a tablespoonful at a time. Mary had to extend her healing, because many of the children were getting pneumonia in the Montana winter.

From the very first day she arrived, the mission belonged to Mary Fields. She would paint, do carpentry, and as soon as the snow melted she started her garden and hennery. Her room was a small one between the Ursulines' cells and the girls' room. Mother Amadeus would say, "Many strange smells come from that room, between your herbs, medicines, and tobacco." But the nun felt that as Mary had been to the convent in Ohio, so now she was to the mission in Montana—a Godsend. Mother Amadeus only wished she could get Mary to stop smoking and drinking. But Mary would say to her over and over, "You take me, you take my smoking and drinking."

In the spring one of the first things Mary did was to build herself a room on the back of the cabin. She told Mother Amadeus she couldn't be in a building with so many people; she needed her own area. She surprised everyone with how nice it was; it even had wood floors.

One of the first lessons Mary taught everyone at the mission was how to pick and dry larkspur. The flowers and leaves would be put into straw mattresses to kill and keep away lice, which were a big problem at the mission.

There were two fears the mission had about Mary when she first arrived. The first was that she might be a female equivalent of the Métis leader, Louis Riel, since she was such a strong, independent-minded person; but from the first day they could see she had only the mission at heart. The second fear was that this big black woman who smoked might scare the girls, since they had never seen a black woman before. But Mary with her gentleness was very soon respected and loved by all.

As her tasks grew, Mary made sure the cabins were kept clean and repaired. She worked with the Jesuit brothers in making beds, chairs, and other furniture and stuffing mattresses with straw, making sure all had larkspur in them. At the same time she was enlarging her hennery and preparing more land for her garden. Mary was becoming a trader among the local farmers. She would trade eggs and butter for lumber, smoked meats, skins, or any item the mission was short of.

Mary had her own lessons to learn. One thing she learned from the very first was that her dresses wouldn't work in Montana. She noticed that the brothers had taken to wearing buckskin. Mary was able to purchase some and made herself a buckskin dress; it was just the thing.

Mary wanted to tan her own skins. She had learned one way to tan skins on the farm in Tennessee, but she liked the color and feel of the Indian buckskin. So she found a Blackfoot Indian woman to show her how to tan skins. She was taken through the process step by step, and wrote it all down. The process went something like this:

First the skin must be fleshed. Mary would lay the skin on a smooth log and scrape all the meat, fat, and membranes off. She would trim the rough edges and the ends of the legs, so the skin had a nice symmetrical shape. With a shaped knifepoint she would make small cuts about 1/2" from the edge of the skin and hook it onto a frame to stretch for drying.

After the skin was dry, the hair and outermost skin and membrane were scraped off. If the epidermis was completely removed, the skin would be softer.

Then she would make a solution of deer brain in warm water, smashing the brain to a fine, pasty consistency and adding water to make enough solution to cover the skin. She would agitate the skins in the solution and get all parts wet. As the skin became saturated, it would become very limp and flexible.

Next she would pull the skin out of the solution, wrap it around a tree, and twist, wringing the skin over a bucket. She would then submerge the skin again and wring it out again, seven or eight times in all, until the skin absorbed all the oil from the brain solution.

Finally, she would take the skin out of the solution and stretch it over a fence rail, pulling and stretching until it was completely dry. The result would be a soft, milky-white buckskin.

Mary was resourceful; she made a skirt and a big blouse. She had no pattern; she simply had someone hold the skin up to her body and mark where the neck, shoulders, and armholes would be, allowing plenty of room to get the garment on and off. She punched holes in the edges of the pieces and laced them together with strips of leather. She learned that in hot weather the ties could easily be undone to allow ventilation through the clothes. This would become her dress for Montana.

Mary also still made all her underclothes the way her mother had taught her, out of flour sacks. The sacks had to be bleached, cut, and sewn. This was the material for all "bloomers," or as the slaves would say, "them funny trousers from flour sacks that gathered at the knees." The brassieres were also flour-sack bands with cups to support the breasts. One thing Mary would never put on again were those petticoats made from muslin, the same stuff that they used back on the farm for sheets. The other stuff they used was calico that made her scratchy. All her petticoats would become rags.

She did have her boots made in Helena. She said she could make her clothes, but the shoes were too much.

It took Mary two to three hides to make her dress. It wasn't long before she was asking the farmers to save her the deerskins along with the meat given to the mission. She would also ask them to save the brains of the deer. One deerskin used one deer brain. The sisters would watch as Mary tanned her skins the way the Blackfoot woman had taught her.

Mary's role as a healer grew; she was treating the nuns, Jesuits, brothers, and the schoolgirls and boys. She told Mother Amadeus that her larkspur was a good medicine. She would always use only the leaves and flowers. Mary boiled these to make a poultice for stomach and intestinal problems, and used the liquid from the boiled larkspur to make a wash for cuts. Mary had learned back on the farm from the old healer how to boil and prepare certain amounts for lung problems, pleurisy, headaches, worms, chronic coughs, toothaches, and, with all those sisters and young girls, female sickness.

CHAPTER TEN

Mary Fields Meets Mary Wells

IN AUGUST OF 1885, a new school year was about to start. The children, both Indian and white, were returning to St. Peter's Mission. In the returning group were three children of one family, two boys and a girl. The boys, Lee Roy and William Wells, had been at the mission for a couple of years, but the girl, Mary, was new. The children's father was a wealthy rancher and trader who wanted a mission education for his children.

Mary Wells looked so small with her big brown eyes and long black curly hair. She was seven years old and would be eight on September 12. When the children arrived at the mission school, the boys and girls were separated and were not allowed to mix at any time. So Mary would be separated from her brothers.

Most of the new girls showed some fear of Mary Fields, but Mary Wells, even though she was very shy, walked right up to her. She looked up at the large black woman with her big brown eyes and said, "We saw many people like you on our trip to Florida and my father had a man on our ranch same color as you." Mary Fields just looked at the bright-eyed little girl, smiled, and patted her on the head.

What amazed Mary Wells was seeing this black woman in Indian buckskin dress, which was made the same way her mother had made her clothes.

Miss Fields took an instant liking to this little girl. "What is your name, child?"

"Mary Wells. I have two brothers here at the school."

Miss Fields said, "Maybe us Marys gonna have to stick together."

The two Marys did form an instant friendship; when Mary Wells wasn't busy with school and her chores she would follow Mary Fields, helping her with her chores. The little girl told Mary that her mother was an A'aninin Indian, whom the whites called Gros Ventre. Mary responded that she was from Africa and didn't know her tribe. Her grandparents had been brought to America as slaves, and she herself had been a slave on Mother Amadeus's family farm in Tennessee. Now the whites had driven the Indians out before bringing in the slaves. Then came the war, and she was made a free person not belonging to anyone else. She told Mary how she had gone to Ohio to work for the Ursulines and now had come with them to Montana.

One day Mary Wells came crying to Miss Fields. She told her that she had been telling one of the nuns how she had spent the summer with her mother's people in a tepee. The nun got very angry at Mary, saying, "You are white now; you must forget that Indian life. I'll pretend you never said that."

Miss Fields held Mary very close to her. "You are Indian, I is black. We must be proud of that part of us and don't let anyone take that from you." Mary felt so close to Miss Fields at that moment.

Mary Fields went to Mother Amadeus to complain. "Why you nuns want to take what is hers from a person?" Mary explained to Mother Amadeus what had happened to Mary Wells.

Mother Amadeus told her it was the job of the church to take the savage out of the children and make them part of society. Mary became very angry. "You took us savages out of Africa, make slaves out of us so we can learn white man's ways. Maybe white man's ways not that good."

Mary walked out and went to her room, where she took a big shot of corn whiskey and sat smoking her pipe. "That nun pick on that child again, I will turn savage and put her head on a stick in front of my room." The word went around the mission fast: Don't put down any of the children or you will have Mary Fields on your back.

Mary Wells would go to Miss Fields' room just for the smells, the smell of burning sage and the many herbs she was always drying; they were the smells of her home. You could always find at least half-a-dozen skins hanging from the rafters that Miss Fields had tanned, letting everyone know they were "tanned the Indian way."

Those smells were so familiar to Mary Wells; they were the good memories of her family's home on the Judith River. She could see her mother tanning skins for her father's clothes. She would tell Mary Fields about the happy times the family had at the Judith ranch.

SOMEHOW MARY FIELDS got some yams. She told the sisters she was going to make yam pies. It became something everyone wanted to be a part of, so Mary had the nuns and girls in the kitchen. Some were scrubbing the yams while some were baking. She baked the yams until they were soft, and told her helpers to peel them while still hot and mash them with a little butter.

Mary took a big bowl, put in three or four eggs and whipped them with a fork. Then she put in a cup of molasses, sugar, and some grated cinnamon. Next she added a big bunch of smashed yams, one cup of evaporated canned milk, and a cup of cream from the farm. She poured the mixture into some piecrust she had made. As soon as one batch of pies was in the oven, she started more. Every little while she would open the oven and stick a knife in the center of a pie. When the knife came out clean, the pie was done.

The pies were served that night and enjoyed by all—the priests, brothers, boys, nuns, and girls. It was a real treat. Mary felt sure that everyone would be looking for yams so she could make more pies.

CHAPTER ELEVEN

The Wells Family

As Christmas approached, many of the children went home for a couple of weeks. When Mary Wells didn't return after the holiday, Mary Fields went to Mother Amadeus to ask why. She was told that the Wells children's father was very ill and the children might not return to the mission school.

Mary Fields told Mother Amadeus she wanted to take a trip to Fort Benton to see the Wells children. The trip was 75 miles; Mary would go to Cascade and catch a stage to Great Falls, then to Fort Benton. The trip would take about three days and it would be a very cold trip in January.

The second week of January, 1885, Mary Fields hooked up the mission wagon. She had on buckskin pants under her buckskin dress, a big buffalo coat, a scarf around her ears, and a big black hat. She looked twice as big as she was.

Mary put her shotgun in the wagon, climbed up, and started her trip to Cascade. The big problem was to make sure the horse didn't slip on any ice. Mary felt good; it was her first time away from the mission and she could see a little of the country, even if it was all white.

It was fun for her to pick out the landmarks as she went down the mission trail: Lionhead Butte, Birdtail Butte, Haystack Butte, Fishback Butte, Black Butte, and Skull Butte—you could see them all from the trail. When the trail turned right onto the Cascades Trail you could see the last of the buttes, Cascade Butte. Mary was cold, but the smoke of her cigar kept her warm.

When she arrived in Cascade, she found a stable to put up her horse and stored the wagon. She was told the stage would stop at the saloon, which was just a block away. As she walked up the street, she could feel a lot of eyes following her. Mary opened the door to the saloon. The smell was enough to knock a person over: the smell of trappers who hadn't changed in six months, miners who had been frozen out, all mixed with the smoke and stale whiskey. It was also dark, but warm.

Mary saw an empty table in the corner. She sat down, leaning her shotgun against her chair. The bartender came over and she told him, "I'll be waiting for the stage to Great Falls and Fort Benton, get me a whiskey."

"Stage'll be by here in an hour or two. You sure you want a whiskey?" Mary touched the barrel of her old shotgun and said, "Yep, whiskey."

A man came out of the dark. "Mary, what are you doing in Cascade in the middle of winter?"

"Mr. Lewis, I'm going to see a family in Fort Benton, the Wells family, you know James Wells?"

Mr. Lewis had a ranch near the mission and his girls went to the school there; he gave a lot of support. "I sure do, Mary, he used to have a big ranch on the Judith, but I hear he is real sick?"

"That's what Mother Amadeus said, so I thought I would go down and try to help."

Mary's whiskey came, and Mr. Lewis told the bartender he would pay for it. He told Mary he wanted to say he bought the first whiskey for a lady who didn't work in the saloon. He said Mary was probably the first woman allowed to have a drink in a saloon in all of Montana.

Mr. Lewis stayed with Mary until her stage arrived and helped her put her small bag in the luggage compartment. He told her he would see her back at the mission.

The stage was full, and Mary got some strange looks from the two other women passengers—this short black woman all dressed in buckskin and a big buffalo coat. At least she was warm, and she wasn't sure the other ladies were. Mary enjoyed the looks she got from the other passengers.

THE STAGE TO GREAT FALLS followed a route along the Missouri River. Strangely enough, the river was flowing north, but Mary couldn't see much of the flow of the river since most of it was frozen. The trip from Cascade to Great Falls only took about three hours, but it was late afternoon and the stage would be staying overnight changing the team of horses. Great Falls wasn't much of a town, sitting at the fork of the Missouri River and the Sun River where they formed some falls; but again, the falls were frozen over.

At the stage stop was a small sign: "Great Falls founded and named 1883." The women were given one room to sleep in and the men another. The drivers slept in the dining room. The stage stop was clean and the passengers were given water to wash with. Mary was laughing to herself; she could see the other two women didn't want to wash in the same bowl or sleep in the same room with her, but after their dinner of hard beans and yet harder biscuits washed down with terrible coffee, she didn't care. She found a corner bed and was warm and comfortable. It didn't take long for those hard beans to start to work on Mary. Again she was laughing to herself; with those beans she would be able to keep those white ladies awake all night.

The innkeeper started banging a pot around 5:30 A.M.; everyone must be ready to leave by seven. The two white ladies did not eat breakfast; Mary thought the beans the night before were enough for them. They didn't miss much; the breakfast was another very hard biscuit with very greasy gravy and the same terrible coffee. Mary kept her humor thinking about those two white women who wouldn't talk to her or give their names, but had to use the same chamber pot as she did, and she got to it first.

The trip to Fort Benton would take another six hours, with a couple of rest stops along the trail. The trail went along a mesa with flat land to the left and a drop off to the Missouri River on the right. When the stage turned off to the right, they could see Fort Benton down by the river. The trail was steep and winding, but it was well used.

Mary knew about Fort Benton from the Jesuit priest. It was a small town right on the Missouri River. It had started around 1846 as a fur-trading post, but became the center of navigation on the Missouri River in 1859; upstream river traffic was stopped by the Great Falls. Mary could see piles of freight along the shore. The stage stopped in front of the small saloon.

Mary got out, looked up and down the street, and saw a small hotel with a sign saying, "Rooms." She took the short walk to the hotel and got a room. It was a small room, and it smelled; she put her bag on the bed and a cloud of dust flew up. She went back to the clerk and asked if he knew the Wells family. He did and gave Mary directions to their house. She walked down the streets towards the fort, which wasn't much. She turned right and saw a row of nice, white, well-kept houses. The Wells' would be the third one on the left.

Mary went up to the door and knocked. The door was opened by Mary Wells, and she let out a scream: "Oh, Miss Fields, you are here in Fort Benton! Please come in." Mary's scream brought the rest of the family. The boys knew Mary Fields. The little girl introduced her to her mother, sister Emma, and little brother James, who saw her and ran away and hid.

Maggie, Mary's mother, took the visitor's coat and told her how much Mary had talked about her. They took her into the parlor where their Christmas tree was still standing. Mary Fields had never seen people so excited to see her.

Maggie asked Mary where she was staying, and she told her hostess which hotel. Maggie said she would send Lee Roy down to gather her bags; she must stay with them. Mary felt she would love to stay with the Wells family. Maggie took her into the bedroom to meet her husband, James Wells. He was so sick that Mary could see he was dying, but he was able to take her hand and smile, "You are welcome to stay with us." Mary had told Maggie she had some herbs with her. Maggie told her all the things they had tried, but she felt her husband was ready to go.

Mary was put in a room with the two little girls. Little Mary gave their guest her bed and made a bed for herself on the floor. The next five days Mary Fields spent helping Maggie take care of Jim. They talked a lot about their lives. The more they talked, the more they discovered their lives were the same.

After the fifth day Mary Fields told Maggie she must get back to her mission and would check and make sure she could catch the stage the next day. Mary asked Maggie if she could bless Jim, and Maggie said she would like that.

Mary prepared some sage with other herbs to burn and lit her pipe. She started to move around Jim, blowing smoke at him and praying in an African language Maggie couldn't understand. Jim just smiled at all the attention he was receiving. Mary knew he couldn't last many more days. He had been a good husband and provided well for Maggie and the children. Mary put her hands on Jim's head and gently rocked back and forth, praying almost in a trance. Jim spoke to Maggie, saying how relaxed he was and that he could breathe for the first time in weeks. Mary smiled at Jim, and he took her hand and thanked her.

That night after dinner, Maggie told Mary she had a favor to ask of her. She told Mary that Senator T. C. Power was in charge of Jim's property, since she as an Indian couldn't own property. Maggie didn't trust him; she feared she would be sent to the reservation and the children to St. Peter's. She asked Mary to please watch out for her children. Maggie's request to T. C. Power would be to remain in Fort Benton with Emma and James; this was also her husband's wish. Mary Fields held Maggie very close and promised she would watch her children, whichever ones were sent to St. Peter's.

The next morning Mary said good-bye to James Wells and the whole family walked her to the stage. As the stage left she could see there were tears in Maggie's eyes, as there were in her own.

Chapter Twelve

From White to Indian

THE TRIP BACK WAS UNEVENTFUL, and Mary's horse and wagon were waiting for her in Cascade. It felt good to be alone on the ride from Cascade to the mission. She could think of the Wells family and how much she had enjoyed being a part of it.

After she put the horse and wagon away at the mission, Mary went to see Mother Amadeus. She told her about the trip and that she felt that Mr. Wells didn't have much longer to live and the children would be staying at home. Mother Amadeus already knew what was going on, since she had received a letter from John Power, T. C. Power's brother.

Mary got right back into her chores, making sure her animals had been taken care of while she was gone. It was so cold and a wind had been blowing, making the air even colder.

In February Mother Amadeus received a letter from Mr. John Power telling her that Maggie Wells would be returning to the reservation with her youngest son, James, and the other four children would be sent back to the mission. He enclosed a copy of James Wells' obituary from the River Press:

February 11, 1885
Death of James Wells
We are called upon to chronicle the death of one of our most esteemed and respected citizens. James Wells passed away this morning at 6 o'clock after a long and painful sickness. His death was not unexpected, as for the past year no hopes have been entertained for his recovery, although until within a short time he had been buoyed up with the idea that he would yet recover. For several weeks he had been confined to his house. The following particulars relative to Mr. Wells were furnished by Mr. John W. Power (brother of T. C. Power) and others who have known him long and intimately. He was born in Indiana about 1840 and was therefore about 45 years of age. When he came west we could not learn, but he was in California and Oregon in early years and came to Montana in 1865 or 66.

In 1868 he had a trading post on Milk River, about twenty miles above old Fort Browning. The following year he entered into the employ of T. C. Power and Bro. and served them in different capacities until the winter of 1874 when they established a post on Milk River, near Black Butte.

Wells was placed in charge. The following fall he relieved T. J. Bogy at Fort Clagett, purchasing an interest in the post which he retained until last year, when he sold out to G. R. Norris. He was one of the noblest men that ever came to this country, generous to a fault; the soul of honor. And will be sadly missed by his old-time friends and associates. He leaves a family of five children who are left amply provided for.

When Mary Fields read the letter, the first thing she noticed was that there was no acknowledgment that James Wells had a wife by the name of Maggie Wells. Mary looked at Mother

Amadeus and said, "That bastard Mr. Power, he do everything Maggie feared, he a real bastard."

"Mary, you can't speak that way."

"Yes I can, he a bastard. He got a wife in Helena and a Gros Ventre wife with a child in Fort Benton, Maggie told me."

"Mary, calm down." Mother Amadeus took her hand.

"I shoot him if he come to the mission."

"No, Mary, you wouldn't."

"Yes I would, Mother, he hurt them babies and Maggie, I shoot him."

Mary went out to her room and had a couple of drinks of her whiskey and a good cigar. She kept saying to herself, "Yes, I shoot his ass, I shoot that Mr. Power." For days Mary remained mad and everyone stayed out of her way.

Within a week the stage came to the mission bringing the four Wells children. The boys were sent over to the boys' area, and the girls were taken in to see Mother Amadeus. Mary and Emma would now live with the Indian children. They would no longer be treated as whites. Mary Fields helped the two girls make their bed; they would sleep together.

Miss Fields had to stand by that first night as the girls' hair was cut off. According to school policy, all Indian girls must have short hair and be bathed in sheep dip, a strong disinfectant. Mary Wells had beautiful long, curly black hair.

Miss Fields watched as Mary's hair fell to the dirt floor. The girl started to cry. Then a rough hand grabbed Mary's chin and pulled her face around. "Pride is a sin, so stop that noise, child, or you will be given something to really cry about."

Mary Fields grabbed the nun's hand. "You touch that child again, I beat you."

The next thing Mary Fields saw was the sister removing the medicine bags from around the Indian girls' necks.

"Sister, what you doing?"

"Mary, they are pagan, idolatrous symbols that must be removed."

"Sister, I got ju-ju around my neck put there by my mama. You got them medals and thing you call a scapular around your neck."

"But mine represent God and His saints."

"Yeah, mine and the Indian girls' represent our ancestors, who we are descended from, and like your saints protect us and tell that Great Spirit to take care of us. So sister, you say our saints and spirits not the same?"

"Mary," the sister replied, "sometimes I'm not sure if you are a Catholic or still part of your African religion."

"Sister, sometimes I'm not sure when I see some of the things you do, but I do hope we all got the same God."

Mary Fields could remember so clearly how her mother would work, braiding her hair interlocked with colorful ribbons; she was so proud of her hair. Then when Mary was fourteen years old she had to cut her hair very short and wear a rag on her head. She could remember being embarrassed looking at herself in a mirror with the short hair, which she never grew long again. Maybe, she thought, that's why she always wore a hat, so no one could see her head.

The sister went to Mother Amadeus to complain about Mary Fields and her threats and the way she was talking about the saints and God. Mother Amadeus smiled at the nun. "Mary Fields is like a mother hen and the Wells children are her care. Do not cross Mary." The nun felt that Mary was protecting the children and Mother Amadeus was protecting Mary, so she'd better stay out of Mary's way.

The beds for the Indians were very crude, with straw mats and old, but very clean, blankets folded at the foot of the bed.

Mary was keeping close watch on the Indian girls. Two Blackfoot girls started to speak in their native language. The nun slapped both girls across the face. "No Indian talk, if you do I'll beat it out of you. You speak English only, you hear?"

Mary had a hard time holding back her temper, but didn't want to cause any more trouble that day. She made the Indian girls' dinner of corn mush, bread and milk.

When she went into the sleeping room she saw Mary Wells in bed, holding Emma in her arms, crying. Miss Fields touched Mary's hand. "It's all right, child, old Mary watch out for you."

A couple of days later Mary Wells came to Mary Fields and told her that Mother Amadeus had asked her to help teach the younger girls. In the fall, she had been with the white students, but now she was treated as an Indian. The students laughed at her because her hair was short and she had to live with the Indians and wear funny clothes. Miss Fields told her to be proud; she was the one teaching because she was so smart and not the white girls. Miss Fields told Mary not to let anyone put her down, because she was the smartest and most beautiful girl at St. Peter's Mission. A big smile spread across the girl's face. "You keep that smile, you don't let anyone take that from you."

AS SOON AS THE GROUND WAS WARM, Mary Fields was out planting her garden. She had some new seeds to try—she was determined to try everything to find out what grew best in Montana. She had also sat some of her hens on eggs and they were hatching lots of chicks.

When Mary Wells wasn't busy she would spend hours with Miss Fields, with Emma always at her side. She told Miss Fields she had written many letters to Mr. Power, asking to be allowed to visit her mother for the summer. Mother Amadeus finally got a letter from Mr. Power stating he didn't want any of the Wells children to see their mother; he didn't want them to become "wild Indians again."

It was hard for Mary Fields to hold back her anger; she would talk to Mother Amadeus and ask, "How come that man do this to such small children?" Mother Amadeus would explain over and over again that he was the executor of James Wells' will and had full power.

Mary would say, "He a slave master, take children from their mother. Slavery supposed to be finished, but not for those Indian children."

"Mary, the Indian children aren't slaves, they are here to be educated so they can move into the white Christian world."

"Then let their mother help. She is a very smart, loving mother."

"Mary, I have no power over that."

"Well, couldn't you have some of the Jesuit fathers talk to him?"

"No, Mary, the children will stay with us this summer."

Mary Fields felt all she could do was to protect the Wells girls and give them her love. As it turned out, she was happy to have Mary and Emma to help her that summer, since she had to help with the new building, run the hennery with about four hundred hens and ducks, and raise a splendid kitchen garden with vegetables for the nuns and Indian girls.

IN JULY 1887, many people came to watch the first stakes being driven by Father Bandini and Mother Amadeus to mark off the foundation for the new convent, a much-wanted and greatly needed building for the sisters.

The Reverend Father Joseph Vincent Francis Damiani, S.J., the superior of St. Peter's Mission, was given a list by Mother

Amadeus to be placed in the cornerstone. This list Mary Wells happened to see.

First Pupils at Ursuline Academy
St. Peter's Mission, Montana

Mollie Lewis, daughter of Ed Lewis
Martha and Annie Brown, daughters of John Brown
Julie Wiegand, daughter of George Wiegand
Louise and Millie Ford, daughters of Sam Ford
Alice, Rose and Laura Aubrey, daughters of Charles Aubrey
Agnes and Babe Moran, daughters of Mr. H. Moran
Clara Davis, daughter of Clara Davis
Louisa Miller, daughter of Mrs. H. Miller
Katie Hines, daughter of John Hines
Mary Reed, daughter of Mrs. Margaret Reed (Pat Connelly)
Katie Pambrun, daughter of A. Pambrun
Mamie Furman, daughter of Coby Furman
Sadie Smith, daughter of George V. Smith
Marguerite Connelly, daughter of George V. Smith
Anna Quigley, daughter of J. R. Quigley
Lily Conrad, daughter of Mrs. J. D. Conrad
Alice Burd, daughter of S. C. Burd
Miss Curran, daughter of Mrs. M. Curran
R. Ferris, daughter of Mrs. J. Hensley

Indians
To 1886—Boys 15, Girls 14
To 1887—Boys 25, Girls 35

Mary Fields found Mary Wells crying behind the hennery. "What's the matter, Mary?"

"My name, my brothers' names and my sister Emma's aren't even on the list. The family of James Wells is just numbers. Miss Fields," Mary went on, "I'm not even counted as a human."

Miss Fields took Mary in her arms. "Mary," she said, "I'm colored. I was born in Tennessee, my mother was a slave, and I never knew my father because he was sold to a farmer in Mississippi or somewhere. I was given my freedom with the emancipation. I was lost, so I went north to Toledo, Ohio. I was given a job with the nuns. But my name was never on the list either."

Mary listened carefully as Miss Fields went on. "I became a Catholic and have worked with the nuns ever since. So, Mary, I'm free, you're free, and who cares if your name is on a list or not. Just be a good proud person. If you have a problem, always come to me." Mary gave Miss Fields a big hug. "Thank you," she whispered.

Mary Wells felt very sad for Miss Fields, being taken from her father; yet Mary wasn't allowed to visit her own mother. One day Mary saw a list of Indian girls, all of whom were Blackfoot-Kaminike: Rose Couquette, Mary Grant, Josephine Couqette, Elizabeth Couqette, Josephine Langolis, Mona Tokomiski, and Susie Russell. It didn't list all the Indian girls, and again, neither Mary nor Emma Wells. But it did mention that "only two can read and write." One of these was Mary.

IN AUGUST OF 1887, Father Lindesmith visited St. Peter's. He brought a lot of joy to all the nuns at the mission; he had been instrumental in bringing the Ursulines to Montana and was very interested in their work there.

Father Lindesmith was a happy man and good to all the children. He didn't seem to notice whether they were white or Indian. He had a laugh that could be heard throughout the mission. He was interested in Miss Fields' hennery and decided that he wanted to put one in every mission.

Everyone listened as Miss Fields told Father Lindesmith about how one night she had to beat to death a polecat that had invaded the chicken coop and killed sixty-two hens. Miss Fields said that it took days to get rid of the smell of the polecat, which sprayed everything as she killed it. Father Lindesmith laughed at her story, and the more he laughed, the more she dramatized the killing of the polecat.

The new building at St. Peter's was finished, with Mary acting as foreman, by late August. From the very first day it was called the Opera House, because it did look like the opera houses in all the towns. It had separate rooms or cells for each of the nuns, a wing for the Indian girls and a wing for the white girls, one large room for dining and a new kitchen. Mary Fields wouldn't move. She said she liked her room behind the log cabin: it was private and she could smoke there.

At this time, the sisters living at St. Peter's included Mother Amadeus, Sister Francis, Sister Mary of the Angels, Sister Thomas, Sister Mary, Sister Martha, Sister Helena, Sister Marguerite, and Miss Wiegand, a postulant. Eighty-nine Indian boys and girls lived at the mission at this time.

Another visitor that summer was Father Fredrick Eberschweiler. Father Eberschweiler was born in the Rhine Province of Germany at Wascweiler in 1841. He and his brother entered the Jesuit novitiate in Westphalia and Father Fredrick was ordained a priest at Maria-Laach. After serving in the army as chaplain, he came to the United States, and spent some time in Buffalo, New York.

Father Eberschweiler was a professor at St. Mary's Seminary in Cleveland from 1871 to 1873. He was then sent to Toledo, where he was assistant at St. Mary's Church from 1873 to 1881. Back in Cleveland, he was stationed at St. Mary's Cathedral from 1881 to 1882.

In August 1883, he came to the Rocky Mountain Missions and was assigned to Fort Benton, with all the surrounding territory as his mission. Father went to Fort Belknap as a missionary to the Gros Ventres and Assiniboine Indians on December 2, 1885. Two years later, in 1887, he left the Fort to stay at the mission he founded for these Indians in the Little Rockies.

When he visited St. Peter's, Father Eberschweiler asked the sisters to open another Ursuline school, St. Paul's Mission, for the Gros Ventre and Assiniboine on the Fort Belknap Reservation. Mary Fields worried that she might be sent to start a garden and hennery for the new St. Paul's Mission.

When Father Eberschweiler returned in the fall, he asked Mother Amadeus if she had decided which sisters would be sent to St. Paul's Mission and whether she might send Mary Fields. Mother Amadeus said she had put a lot of thought into it and she would send two sisters, Sister Francis and Sister Martha. Mother Amadeus said she couldn't send Mary since she was needed there at St. Peter's, and she felt that only she could control Mary—if only a little.

Father Eberschweiler asked Mother Amadeus how soon the sisters could leave. She said she had talked to them and they could leave in a couple of days. Mary packed the sisters a lunch basket as they left in a lumber wagon for a ranch where they would stay overnight. The stage route ran past the ranch, which was on Shaw Butte. The following morning they would take a stage to Fort Benton.

When Sister Francis wrote back to Mother Amadeus about their trip, she always shared the letters with Mary Fields. The sisters had stayed overnight at the Brown ranch and caught the stage for Fort Benton, but on the way the stage stopped in Great Falls at the Park Hotel to throw out a drunken passenger who refused to stop swearing in front of the sisters.

They spent the night at Fort Benton, taking another stage to Fort Assiniboine, where they would spend the night with the commander's family. The wife was depressed and a little crazy. Their daughter had recently been killed in a fall from a horse, and she blamed the Indians, who she said had scared the horse. She kept saying to the sisters, "How can you be going out into outlaw, Indian territory to teach?"

The next morning the sisters were to go as far as O'Hanlon's Ranch, where they would be met by the Indians from St. Paul's Mission. The following day several wagonloads of Indians came to welcome the sisters, but they wouldn't leave for the mission until they saw the great engine. This was the engine of the train that traveled from east to west in Northern Montana. The blankets were spread out along the tracks and the Indians had a picnic of dried meat, fruit, and many items not familiar to the sisters. All the food was shared with them.

The train came, blew its whistle, spewed out big clouds of smoke, and passed on. The Indians stood impassive, watching the train go by, then packed their belongings back into the wagons, told the sisters where to sit, and set out on their way. They arrived at St. Paul's on September 14.

CHAPTER THIRTEEN

Tragedy at the Mission

Miss Fields' room was always filled with the scent of wild sage. She would say that the smoke was good for her body and spirit, the exact words spoken by Mary Wells' mother. How could people from such distant cultures, one from Tennessee and one from Montana, one black and one Indian, be so much alike? When Miss Fields spoke, Mary could always hear her mother's voice. Miss Fields would hold the girl in her arms and say to her, "Mary, you think too much: your head is going to pop."

Mary Fields was pleased that Sister Marguerite had taken a liking to the Wells girls; she had found them extra blankets and pillows since the girls were still sleeping together.

During that summer of 1887, the children who couldn't go home would help in the garden or kitchen or with the farm animals. The boys and girls were allowed to mix a little, on picnics or in some of the chores. Now Mary could see more of her brothers, who were working with the cattle and cutting hay.

One hot afternoon in September, Mary's older brother Lee Roy was badly injured. Sister Marguerite took Mary to the boys' school where Lee Roy, pale and unconscious, was spread out on a clean bed. He had been stacking hay and was on top of the pile. He was told to slide down for lunch, and when he did, he slid right into a pitchfork that had been left against the pile with its tongs up. The pitchfork had pierced Lee Roy's abdomen.

Mary was allowed to stay near her brother. William and Emma were also brought to Lee's bedside. The doctor arrived quickly and spent a lot of time with Lee Roy. Sister Marguerite brought Father Eberschweiler and Brother Claessens. "Your brother is very sick and will probably die," Father Eberschweiler told Mary. "He is in God's hands."

Both Marys trusted Father Eberschweiler, since they knew him from his many visits. The children were all allowed in the room while Lee Roy was given the last rites of the Catholic Church. As Mary prayed the "Our Father," she could feel the strong hand of Mary Fields on her shoulder.

> Our Father, who art in heaven, hallowed be Thy name.
> Thy kingdom come.
> Thy will be done on earth as it is in heaven.
> Give us this day our daily bread,
> and forgive us our trespasses,
> as we forgive those who trespass against us.
> And lead us not into temptation, but deliver us from evil.
> Amen.

Mary had said this prayer over and over, but it didn't really mean much to her. "Hallowed be Thy name"? "Lead us not into temptation"? Where was her mind going?

Mary knew she had to be a witness to death once again. She had seen her father die, but here was this young strong person, her brother, who was dying. The doctor, the priest, and the nuns all kept saying over and over, "It's in God's hands." Mary could only think, "Whose God? What God? Why couldn't they bring a medicine man? They must do something, not just stand back and keep saying over and over again, 'It's in God's hands.'"

This would be Mary's first fight alone with death. She didn't know where to turn. She could hear her mother explaining to her, "Mary, the A'aninin value life highly and always pray for a very long life, but our people know when they are about to die and are ready to resign themselves, knowing that the family is there to ease their last moments. We must see to it that our people are surrounded by family. The family members must make sure that all the proper last steps are taken."

Mary kept hearing the prayer her mother had taught her:

> O Great Spirit, whose voice I hear in the winds, and whose breath gives life to the entire world, hear me! I am small and weak. I need your strength and wisdom. Let me walk in beauty and make my eyes ever behold the red and purple sunset. Make my hands respect the things you have made, and sharpen my ears to hear your voice. Make me wise so that I may understand the things you have taught my people. Let me learn the lessons you have hidden in every leaf and rock. I seek strength, not to be greater than my brother, but to fight my greatest enemy—myself. Make me always ready to come to you with clean hands and straight eyes. So when life fades, as fading sunset, my spirit may come to you without shame.

Mary asked Sister Marguerite and Mary Fields to bathe her brother, dress him in his finest clothes, and comb his hair so that he could prepare for death. She wanted to paint his face, but was afraid to ask.

Miss Fields asked Mother Superior if she could bless Lee Roy. The sisters protested, but Mary Fields persuaded them. In her flamboyant style, she told the nuns she would destroy the mission if they refused, since this was for Mary Wells and not for a bunch of narrow-minded nuns.

Miss Fields went up to Lee Roy's bed, speaking a language no one understood. She puffed on her pipe and blew smoke all over the boy's face, up his nose, in his ears and mouth. She moved in a funny dancing motion, putting her hands all over him and still talking in that strange language. This went on for almost an hour. She finally came over to Mary and said, "His spirit is clean and free; he can go now."

At last, Mary felt peace with her brother's untimely death. She felt that Miss Fields had been the instrument of a powerful, cleansing spirit. A special person had blessed Lee Roy. Mary Fields was surprised at how grown-up Mary was acting during this difficult time.

Another thing Mary knew that she couldn't ask for was to have her brother wrapped in his best blanket, with his body laid on a stretcher, not in a coffin, and placed in a forked tree with his head towards the setting sun. Nevertheless, Mary wanted to do all she could to make Lee Roy's burial as traditional as possible. According to tradition, his face should be covered with a piece of cloth. Mary decided to cover Lee's face with the scarf her mother had given her. The scarf was priceless to her, but obedience to tradition was stronger than sentiment, so Mary was willing to part with it.

Lee Roy survived for three days and died on September 3, 1887, at the age of fifteen. A mass was said with all the children attending who had not left for the summer. Mary had begged everyone to please let her mother know of Lee's accident and death, but Maggie did not appear at the funeral.

Mary and Miss Fields made sure that all Lee Roy's personal things were buried with him—his pocketknife and old pocket watch from his father, and his blanket, a gift from his mother. The nuns objected, but Mary Fields stood with Mary on whatever she wanted to do. Mary had been taught that it is good to cry and mourn the dead, but would not cry because she felt she needed to be strong for Emma.

Lee Roy was buried in a little cemetery near the mission church, in a coffin made by the brothers. A little white cross with the words, "Lee Roy Wells, aged 15, died September 3, 1887," marked his grave.

This was a big loss to William, as he had never before been separated from his brother. The sisters were worried about him and tried to look out for him.

Mary told Mary Fields that she was most hurt that her brother Lee Roy would never be able to do the Sun Dance, known by the Gros Ventres as the Sacrifice Dance. She knew that the white man's law forbade the ceremony, but it was still performed by all young Indians. It had been her mother's wish for her sons to perform this ritual, signifying entry into manhood. Yet, even at her young age, Mary knew that under the pressure of the white man's world Lee Roy never would have been able to do it.

Mary Fields told Mary she must believe that her brother's injury, suffering, and death were his Sacrifice Dance. By the torture he endured, he had proved himself the possessor of the manly qualities of bravery and endurance. He had proved himself a real man and had demonstrated his tribal worth. He would be remembered as a true believer and true Indian. His mother would be proud of her son. Surely, the ancestral grandfathers would be his guardians as he made his way to the next life.

September 12, 1887, was Mary Wells' ninth birthday. Mary Fields made sure the girl had a cake, which she baked herself. She also knitted Mary a scarf. She placed the scarf around her neck and said, "This is from your mother and me. We gonna always be there, giving you a hug around your neck."

CHAPTER FOURTEEN

Growing Pains

THE WINTERS OF 1887 AND '88 were very cold. The children were told to write home and have warm clothes sent. Mary Fields went to Mother Amadeus and asked her to write to Senator Powers and request warm clothes for the Wells children, as it seemed that their letters weren't being answered. She said she would, and shortly warm clothing arrived for them.

The summers were busy, as many children began to stay at St. Peter's. The sisters and Mary Fields took the children on picnics and camping trips. The children loved to picnic in the canyon and to camp by the Dearborn River, which flowed from the main range of the Rocky Mountains to the west of the mission. The water flowed eastward to join the Missouri, cutting a broad fertile valley on which the mission grew its food. The Catholic missionaries did the first serious and productive farming in Montana Territory.

The sisters were sure always to tell the children the stories of the white man clear back to Lewis and Clark. Mary Fields would shake her head and roll her eyes back as the sisters told of how the explorers were the first white men to be in the area in 1804 and had named the river the Dearborn.

Mary Wells tried hard to tell Mary Fields the Indian name for Dearborn River, but she couldn't remember it. She knew the names of many others: Missouri (Big River), Maria (Bear River), Teton (Knee River), Judith (White River), Musselshell (Shell River), and Yellowstone (Elk River). But, as hard as she tried, she couldn't come up with the Indian name for the Dearborn. She knew that the whites had named the Dearborn River for Henry Dearborn, Secretary of War.

Mary also knew that west of Fort Benton, the Missouri River turned sharply to the southwest and flowed through a broad, deeply cut plain that rose gradually toward the main range of the Rocky Mountains. To the west of these mountains, the waters of the Maria, Teton, Sun, and Dearborn Rivers flowed eastward to join the Missouri, cutting broad fertile valleys that the Native Americans had marked as favorite hunting grounds for many generations.

The Army and Indian Administration officers realized early on that the whites would demand the fertile river valleys for their own and would need protection against the dispossessed Indians. Above the mouths of these tributary rivers, the Missouri became smaller and more easily traversed and was a favored crossing for Indians, who used this area for hunting and getting to the southern part of Montana. So, for the whites, control of this area became important to the peace and safety of southern Montana. The Mullan Road also ran squarely through this section for making trips from Fort Benton to Helena. It was in one of these fertile valleys that St. Peter's Mission farm was located.

Sister Marguerite would ask Mary Wells how she knew so much about the area and its rivers. Mary would always respond, "My father was a trader; he knew the area and taught me."

The community of sisters was growing. A number of the girls who had come there as students entered the Ursuline order. Sister Cecelia had been Julia Wiegand. Others came to join them from as far away as Cleveland and Toledo. Sister Agnes had been Mary Dunn. Mary Rose Galvin became Sister Mary Rose. But Mary Wells could never see herself as a person who would enter the Ursuline order.

In the summer of 1888, Mother Amadeus asked Father Eberschweiler to "bring her six girls" from the Gros Ventre country. The request was unusual, since St. Peter's was primarily for Blackfoot Indians. The mission was obviously in need of financial subsidies which could be obtained from the government for the Gros Ventres.

Agessa (her full name was Mary Josephine Agessa) was one of the Gros Ventre girls Father Eberschweiler brought. She had been born near Chinook, Montana, on the site of the old Belknap agency. Her father, Bushy Head, was one of the five underchiefs of the Gros Ventre tribe on the reservation. Agessa and Mary became friends, which gave Mary a chance to ask Agessa's father whether he had known her grandparents. He had known Mary's grandfather, but not her grandmother.

Mary Wells told Mary Fields how good it felt to have other Gros Ventres at the mission—other Indians who would respect her. Agessa was among the favored ones, along with Mary and Emma. Mary thought she was so beautiful, with her high forehead, profusion of straight black hair and perfect white teeth. Why the Ursulines didn't cut her hair, no one knew for sure or would dare ask. Agessa was smart, wrote well, sang, and painted.

Agessa fell ill with pneumonia and died. She was buried near Mary's brother Lee Roy. Bushy Head and his wife were able to get to the mission before Agessa died. Mary told Bushy Head that now there were two A'aninin buried on that hill. Her friend's father took Mary's hand and smiled.

Mary Fields couldn't believe the things Mary Wells had gone through during her young years. The big shock for Mary that summer was that she started to menstruate. She had no idea what was happening to her, since the sisters had never told her this would happen, and she ran to Mary Fields to tell her she thought she was dying. Mary Fields held the girl and said, "It's God's way of making you a woman. Your body will start to change now." She showed Mary how to take care of herself, and told her not to listen to the many stories she would hear.

A short time later Mary came to Miss Fields with a story. One of the Blackfoot girls had taken it upon herself to tell Mary what she understood about sex. She said that to conceive a child one needed to have sex over a period of time; conception could not usually occur as the result of being with a man only once. It was an Indian tradition that many young girls were given in marriage before starting to menstruate. She also said that a girl should not start to menstruate until she had experienced sex.

Mary asked Miss Fields if any of this was true. Miss Fields assured her that it absolutely was not, and in a clear and gentle manner dispelled her concerns. "If you have any questions, Mary, always come to me."

Work on the new stone convent building was underway. Mary Wells got to know some of the workers, since Mary Fields cooked the noon meal for them. The workers started calling Miss Fields "Black Mary." Mary Wells asked her if being called that bothered her. She said, "Names mean nothing to Mary, it's only the way they say it."

Growing Pains

Most of the materials for the new convent came from the surrounding hills. The sandstone was quarried from the hills north of the mission, but the best thing to Mary was the beautiful granite steps that came from Square Butte in the Judith basin. When finished, the convent was three stories high, with a chapel, classrooms, an art room, a conservatory, parlors, and dormitories for the girls, along with a refectory for the nuns and children. The new building, with classrooms that had slate boards and heat, was opened on January 11, 1892.

Then, in March of 1892, the mission ran out of food. Nothing remained but cornmeal. No butter, no eggs, not even a piece of coal or coal oil. And the mission was broke. Things had gotten so bad that as many as thirty boys, along with many brothers and priests, became ill with pneumonia. Father Eberschweiler and several other Jesuits came to help in the crisis.

During this period of very little, the Indian girls survived the best. Miss Fields had a kitchen garden with vegetables for the nuns and Indian girls and could make the most food from practically nothing. When word got out about the mission's plight, supplies finally started to arrive, and by early summer the mission was back to normal.

St. Peter's Mission, 1884

This peaceful valley, reached by a cut-off from the Mullan road, is enclosed on one side by rugged peaks of the Big Belt Range, green with pine and fir, and on the other side with barren rocky hills of rugged shape. The traveler seeing it for the first time experiences delight and surprise at the sudden beauty of it all.

—SISTER GENEVIEVE MCBRIDE, O.S.U.
The Bird Tail, 1974

The church was begun in 1875 and finished the following spring. It was soon too small for the congregation, settlers and halfbreeds, so an addition was built.

—Sister Genevieve McBride, O.S.U.
The Bird Tail, 1974

Mary Fields at St. Peter's Mission, circa 1885

There were years of happy living for Mary, who had no fear of man or beast and could lick two men, it was said.

—Sister Genevieve McBride, O.S.U.
The Bird Tail, 1974

The first boys' school at St. Peter's Mission.
This stone building was erected in 1880.

*The new boys' school, circa 1896.
The old mission and the girls' school are in the background.*

St. Peter's Mission circa 1887

The Ursuline Sisters came from Helena on October 30, 1884; four of them quickly established their school in the best convent tradition, though it must be admitted their log cabin convent and thirty dusky little maidens required certain unexpected adjustments. They lived in their cabins seven years.

—FATHER JOSEPH DAMIANI, S.J.
Jesuits in Montana, 1960

Opposite: *Indian girls at St. Peter's Mission, circa 1884. Mary Wells, left side, large bow in hair; Emma Wells, left, bottom row.*

Corpus Christi. A most beautiful procession—the Mission was decked in flags and flowers. The day was a perfect day. The Mission never looked so beautiful. The little Indian girls who strewed flowers wearing pink dresses and white caps and little baskets strung about their necks with pink ribbons. The other Indian girls wore their blue polka dot dresses.

—SISTER GENEVIEVE MCBRIDE, O.S.U.
The Bird Tail, 1974

The new convent under construction, circa 1890

July 7, 1887, was an eventful day at the Mission. Father Bandini drove the first stake, and Mother Amadeus the last, that was to mark the foundation of the new convent.

—Sister Genevieve McBride, O.S.U.
The Bird Tail, 1974

St. Peter's Mission, circa 1893

In late December 1891, the Ursulines moved into a new three-story stone building which but proved to be a more sturdy shell for the same stark poverty.

—FATHER JOSEPH DAMIANI, S.J.
Jesuits in Montana, 1960

Joseph and Mary's Wedding
July 23, 1895

The interior of the chapel at St. Peter's Mission as it is today —unchanged since 1910.

Mary Fields' headstone.

Chapter Fifteen

Joseph Gump

In May of 1892, the mission hired a handsome young German man named Joseph Oswald Gump to be foreman on the mission farm. Many of the girls at the school did all they could to sneak a look or find a way to run into him. Mary Wells watched him from the window. Joseph was a very shy man, tall and lanky, with an angular face and dark brown hair that he wore combed back and slightly long. The white girls flirted with him openly, but Mary only watched from a distance, certain that he would not be interested in talking to any of the Indian girls.

Miss Fields found out he had been born in Germany on March 23, 1869, which made him just twenty-three years old. To Mary Wells he was old, since she would only be fourteen on September 12. The Jesuits had recruited Joseph Gump in Spokane and, since he spoke German, it would be easy for him to work with the German brothers.

Mary Fields and Joseph Gump became the best of friends from the very first day of his arrival. Joseph was amazed at how Mary could manipulate the nuns in her sometimes quiet, sometimes loud manner.

Mary told Joseph, "I learned a lot as a slave—to say yes'm, ma'am, and then do as I damn well pleased." She told him the story of how she had been a slave for the Dunne farm and was later given her freedom. She was sure of her age, which most slaves weren't; she was sixty years old.

The first thing that amazed Joseph about Mary was that she wore men's buckskin clothes. Also, left over from her plantation days, she had one bad habit that drove the sisters nuts: she still smoked cigars that she rolled by hand from special tobacco that she would send for from somewhere in Tennessee. It wasn't long before Joseph was seen having a smoke with her.

Joseph purchased two six-guns and two shotguns for himself and Mary, since they often traveled to buy supplies, and more and more outlaws were in the area.

Mary was already good with the shotgun. One of the sounds she and Joseph brought to the mission was the sound of the guns as the two of them practiced out in the coulee (the wash on the prairie). Mary found that by carrying her gun in her belt she was becoming a very fast draw.

On September 9, there was a lot of excitement around the mission. Two brothers, John and George Mosney, had been hired for a dollar a day plus their room and board. Mary told the two men what their chores would be. George told Mary he wouldn't take orders from a nigger and would have to show her her place. He took out a whip. Mary grabbed her shotgun. John Mosney grabbed his rifle; it was a standoff, with Mary standing her ground.

Joseph was called, and he told the Mosney brothers there would be "no touching of rifles nor any whipping." He told them Mary Fields was their foreman, but he was going to fire them. They would be paid two days' wages, which was two dollars each. John told Mary he would get her someday. Joseph told him if he was smart he would leave the territory, because he would bet Mary would shoot him and his brother on sight, and she was one "damn good shot."

That evening Mary and Joseph were sitting having a smoke.

"Mary, I never seen you so mad as today. What started you off?"

"Joseph, when I was seventeen or eighteen the Dunnes got a new overseer. A slave ran off but he was caught two days later and brought back to the farm. Mr. Dunne had him tied up with his arm pulled above his head. All the slaves had to come down and watch.

The overseer said, 'You blacks try to flee, I will beat, chain, incarcerate, put you in irons and whip you.' He took that man's shirt off and swung that cowhide, big welts formed on his back, then when the whip strike again they would pop and blood and water would run down his back. That man never scream, his eyes roll back, be all white, but he never screamed, the overseer start sweating he was hitting him so hard.

The slaves were all crying, both women and men. Finally the overseer look at Mr. Dunne, Mr. Dunne nods his head, the whipping stopped and Mr. Dunne left. The other slaves cut the man down and took him to the healer. The healer worked all night, but the man died.

I see a whip pointed at me, I go crazy.

The next day after the man died Mrs. Dunne go crazy, she sent all the house slaves down to the slave quarters. We could hear her screaming at Mr. Dunne, she called him murderer. Told him he was going to hell. That went on for two days. Mr. Dunne fired the overseer, but when we were called back to the house, Mrs. Dunne wouldn't speak to Mr. Dunne. At dinner he sat at one end of the table and her at the other, not one word spoken. The silence in the house went on for months and she was never the same to him after that whipping. I never heard or saw another whipping on the Dunne farm."

Joseph could see where Mary's anger came from; it was very hard to think of spending most of your life as a slave.

Mary told Joseph that among the many causes of slaves running away, perhaps none was more poignant or pervasive than members of families seeking to reunite. Slaves would run to neighboring plantations to be with their husbands or wives. They would run away to search for mothers and fathers, and all too often to look for their children—in vain.

The most traumatic thing was for youngsters to be sold away from their parents. She looked at Joseph with tears in her eyes. "My father was sold away from my mother and me. My mother was never the same."

October 7, 1892, was a big day for the mission. The teachers from Fort Shaw government school visited St. Peter's Mission School to check on the classes there. They said that they were pleased with the teaching methods at St. Peter's, and they especially liked the big slate blackboards and all-new textbooks.

During the teachers' visit, Mary Fields was doing laundry. All the old clothes that couldn't be used anymore were being thrown into a bonfire. Mary didn't realize that some old cartridges had been left in the pocket of a pair of pants, and when the pants went into the fire the cartridges exploded. Everybody ran for cover, but one round hit Sister St. Gertrude near her eyes.

Sister St. Gertrude was taken by wagon into Helena. Even though word came back that she would be all right, Mary felt terrible. She felt as though she had shot Sister St. Gertrude just the same as if she'd used a gun. Sister said it was an accident and could have happened to anyone. Besides, the mission needed a little excitement.

Joseph looked at Mary and started to laugh. He told her she was becoming so fast with her gun she could shoot a nun without even drawing. But Mary got angry with him for laughing at her; she didn't see any humor in this accident.

On October 10, Mr. Madden, a great benefactor to St. Peter's Mission, was killed when he was thrown from his buggy. The family asked the mission if they could build a casket and have Mary Fields help prepare the body. Mary wasn't sure she wanted to do this. But he was a friend who had given much to the mission and she had worked with him on some of the new buildings.

He was buried on October 16 after a High Mass at the mission. Mary Wells and the other children sang at his Mass. It was considered a very sad loss for the mission; he had always provided much needed food.

On October 12, the students celebrated the four-hundredth anniversary of the discovery of America by Columbus. Mary helped the children put on a play, after which they all went on a picnic to Mt. Ursula, where they sang and played games. Mary Wells couldn't help thinking about how Columbus Day actually celebrated something deeply important to her very existence—the day the destruction of her culture at the hands of the white man began.

As for Mr. Christopher Columbus, who had sailed from Spain with his three ships—Santa Maria, Pinta, and Niña—and had landed on San Salvador Island on October 12, 1492, saying he had discovered a new land to be called America—how can someone discover a place that is already inhabited by humans? Of course, the whites never thought of the Indians as fully human beings, but saw them as savages and continued to treat them as such.

So, although Mary felt moved to celebrate Columbus Day for her father's sake, despite knowing very little about his heritage other than that he was white, she still grieved this day for her mother's people.

Mary asked Miss Fields to explain slavery to her. Miss Fields told her that the first African slaves were brought to America in 1619 to work the plantations in the warmer climates of the South. Slavery became the basis of the plantation economy, but it was confined to the South because anti-slavery sentiment rose in the North and was made a burning issue by the abolitionists.

Most serious clashes in the period 1820–1860 were between the South and the North and hinged on the question of the extension of slavery to new territories. The matter did not end until Abraham Lincoln's Emancipation Proclamation in 1863 and the North's victory in the Civil War, which freed all slaves.

When Mary asked Miss Fields whether she felt the Negroes and Indians would ever be really free, Miss Fields answered, "No." She said that we are all equal in God's eyes, but not that equal in the eyes of the whites. "Just look how different the white girls are treated from the Indian girls by nuns who say we are all equal." Mary loved Miss Fields so much and knew she could ask her anything.

That evening Mary Fields was sitting with Joseph. "That Mary Wells' head going all the time, she wanna know everything."

"Mary, tell me more about slavery on the farms in Tennessee."

Joseph Gump

"Joseph, there was always fear and worry among the slaves. All the farms the same: the slaves watch, listen and wait in that tiny world of the farm. They know right away about anything wrong in the masters' families. It's like you and me know everything about the nuns, priests and brothers, the slaves knew when the master drink to excess, have health problems, I knew when the master and missus not getting along. The slaves see all the arguing, anger, jealousy, and hatred in the family. The slave sees and knows it all.

The big problem was the masters sleeping with slave women; this made many slaves run away. Masters' wives could be murderous toward black women they thought might be sleeping with their husbands."

"Mary, it is so hard for me to understand slavery."

"Joseph, just look around at the Indians, you see worse than slavery, the whites just want them to vanish. Look at the Wells children, they are a product of a white man and an Indian. Now they in no world—at least I'm free."

A couple of days after the Columbus Day celebration, Mary drove Sisters St. Catherine and Angela to Sun River and Fort Shaw to beg Dr. Newman to pull Sister St. Catherine's tooth. Dr. Newman refused to pull the tooth because he didn't have the right forceps. On their way back, the women got lost. Mary couldn't figure out how she could get lost, since she knew the area and all the buttes.

At the foot of Crown Butte, they found a cabin owned by a friend, Mr. Farrell, who got a good laugh at seeing this large black woman in buckskins along with a couple of nuns lost out on the prairie. Mr. Farrell had recently married a former student of the mission, Miss Whitefield; he was happy to help out. He got in his wagon and had Mary and the nuns follow him back to the mission. The nuns said they would offer a special prayer for him.

Sister St. Catherine's tooth was still bothering her, so on October 25, Mary again loaded Sister Angela and Sister St. Catherine in the wagon for the trip to Great Falls to have the tooth extracted. The tooth was pulled and they were all to spend the night at the new hospital run by the Sisters of Providence, who were friends of the Ursuline Sisters. Mary was fed well and given a room that was used for patients. She slept well.

On the trip back Mary wanted to laugh at Sister St. Catherine—her face was all swollen and black and blue, she looked like she had been in a fight. Sister St. Catherine didn't say much but would let out a weird sound every time the wagon hit a bump or a hole in the trail, of which there were many.

November 10 was a historic day at St. Peter's Mission. The new coal fire furnace had been lit, and everybody enjoyed the heat it produced. The coal had been delivered at Cascade for $5.50 a ton. But with the new coal furnace came a big problem. Joseph had sent one of the farmhands over to shovel coal. The farmhand had told Joseph that "Black Mary" (his name for Miss Fields) should shovel the coal, since the black dust wouldn't show on her.

Joseph could feel his anger rise. He hit the man and immediately fired him. Joseph called a meeting of all the men at the mission, reminding them that, although a woman, Miss Fields was also a foreman and that they must respect her or get off the mission. Joseph's anger was so strong that he finished with, "In fact, I'll personally take care of the next person who shows a lack of respect."

The next time Miss Fields saw Joseph, she gave him a big bear hug. "Joseph," she said, "you are a wonderful person, but I can take care of myself, and you have trouble killing a chicken."

Mary and Miss Fields spent hours talking about their traditions. So many of Mary's memories were fading.

Miss Fields would never miss an opportunity to mention Mary Wells to Joseph, whose response was always the same: "I'm too old for her." Miss Fields would always come back with, "On the farm, a girl is never too young and a man never too old." Nor would she miss an opportunity to tease Mary about that "good-looking German foreman Joseph."

In December two Blackfoot Indian girls, Francesca Sleeping Bear and Susie Land, ran away. They wanted to return to their families. The girls were found the next day half-frozen, hiding in a haystack at the Morris horse ranch, and were returned to the mission. They were spanked and ordered to go without dinner for two nights.

Mary Fields went to Mother Amadeus and told her no child should be hit, only loved. If they were loved they wouldn't run away. Mother Amadeus told Mary that spanking was necessary in training a child. Mary stormed out, went to her cabin and had a drink. That night and the next she made sure the two girls had dinner, not caring if the nuns knew.

Still mad the next day, Miss Fields shot an eagle that was trying to steal her chickens. She hit the thief on its wing as it was flying. She thought she had a real trophy, but Mary Wells informed her otherwise. Mary told Miss Fields that she must take care of the eagle, because it would be bad luck to kill it. The eagle was taken to Joseph.

Joseph put a sack over its head and repaired the wing as best he could, but he told Mary Fields that it would never fly again.

"Now I got another mouth to feed and he don't like me, he just hiss at me."

"He will become tame for you, Mary."

"No, Joseph, I don't like that bird, he eat my chickens."

CHAPTER SIXTEEN

Mary Plays Matchmaker

January of 1893 was bitter cold, with temperatures as low as 39° below zero at St. Peter's and 50° below in Helena. Mother Francis became ill with pneumonia and was confined to her cell.

Mary Wells and many of the other Indian children also became ill with pneumonia. Dr. Newman came to see Mother Francis and the sick children. He said that the buildings must be kept warmer, but the mission was low on coal and wood because of the cold weather, and the sisters were afraid to use up what little they had.

By the first of February the woodpile was very low, and it was too cold to go into the mountains to cut more wood. Mother Amadeus gathered all the girls, both white and Indian, into one room and all the nuns into another to save what little fuel was left.

Mary Fields was trying all her herbs, but it seemed that nothing worked. Dr. Newman told Mary she was doing everything right, but they must find more fuel to keep everyone warm. All they could hope for was a change in the weather.

One day, Father Markham's chimney caught fire. The girls all saw the blaze and smoke coming from his cabin. When word was rushed to him about the fire, Father Markham came running over to the girls' cabin inquiring where their fire was.

They had never before seen a priest so excited. Sister Anna told him the fire was in his own house, in his chimney. Father Markham ran back, but Joseph, Mary Fields, and some others from the farm had already put the fire out.

One cold evening late in February, the boys came over to entertain the girls with a play for Washington's birthday. Mary was happy to see her brother. She was surprised when Joseph Gump sat next to her and asked her name, as if he didn't know it. The sisters and the other girls teased her later that night. One of the white girls said to her, "I'll bet you he doesn't know you're an Indian. I'll make sure he finds out." The teasing made Mary cry but, as always, Miss Fields was there to defend her, telling the other girls to mind their own business.

About a week later, Mr. Moriarty, the photographer from Helena, arrived to take some photographs of the boys who had failed to show up for pictures on an earlier trip. As Mary Wells served him a meal, he said to her, "Would you like to have a photograph of yourself taken? You're a beautiful young lady."

Mary blushed because Joseph Gump was listening. She told the photographer she would if she could run and find her sister to be in the picture with her. Mary and Emma had their photograph taken together while Joseph Gump watched, and Mr. Moriarty told Mary that he would bring the photograph back with the pictures he had taken of the boys. Mr. Moriarty also took a picture of Mary Fields standing with her shotgun.

Mary Plays Matchmaker

On March 10, 1893, Bishop Brondel, who was bishop for all Montana, paid an unexpected visit to the mission. As soon as Mary Fields saw him she would go the other way. She would tell Joseph over and over again, "I don't like that man and he don't like me!"

"Mary, you just think that."

"No, Joseph, I don't like that man."

"Maybe he doesn't approve of your drinking and smoking."

"No, I just get bad feeling about him."

"Come with me and say hello."

"No, Joseph, I might punch him."

"Mary, you make me laugh."

The bishop had with him the Very Reverend J. M. Cataldo, S.J., who was looking for sisters who wanted to do missionary work in Alaska. The next day the bishop and Father Cataldo left for Helena, but came first to talk to Mother Amadeus.

Mary found Joseph out milking. "Mary, where have you been, they said you didn't fix breakfast for the bishop?"

"Joseph, I don't cook for that man."

"Mary, maybe Father Cataldo will take you to Alaska?"

"Joseph, I stay right here in Montana, these sisters going to bury me here, not Alaska." Mary turned and walked out of the barn talking to herself.

Mary Fields was playing matchmaker every time she got a chance between Mary Wells and Joseph. She missed all the girls when they went home for the summer, especially Mary and Emma Wells.

It was time for Mary and Joseph to sit in the evening and tell stories. Joseph told Mary that he had been born in Oberkreutzberg, Germany, and had come to the United States in 1861, when he was eight years old. His family had settled in

Milwaukee, where his father had worked as a brewmaster. When he was sixteen Joseph moved with his family to Spokane. His father died in 1879, when Joseph was only eighteen. Joseph then took care of his mother until she married a widower, Mr. Sapper, who had two children. Joseph didn't like his stepfather, so he moved to a wheat ranch outside of Spokane, where he worked for the next four years.

One summer he had traveled to Montana and had spoken with a priest in Helena about the missions. When he returned to Spokane, he saw an ad for a foreman at St. Peter's. He answered the ad and was hired.

Mary told Joseph about her early life. "When I was young I stayed in the house all the time. I was there for Mrs. Dunne and Dolly. I loved them because they were good to me. They taught me how to weave, spin, read and write. Before I was very big I could do things no other slaves could do, but I was still a slave.

When we were freed, you hear the old story about forty acres and a mule, it makes me laugh. They sure did tell us that, but I never knowed anyone who got it. The officers tell us we would get slave pension. That just exactly what they tell. They sure did tell me I would get a parcel of ground to farm. Nothing ever hatched out of that, neither."

Joseph told Mary that the stories she told him would remain with him forever. Mary would say to him, "That's a long time, Joseph."

In August, a Father Van Gorp, S.J., who had been appointed Superior General of Rocky Mountain Missions, came to visit St. Peter's. He wanted to talk to Joseph about the farm and to Mary about the hennery. As she kept being told, every one of the missions wanted to start one. Mary told Joseph, "I like this one, he has good questions."

Mary Plays Matchmaker

A couple of evenings later Mary and Joseph were having a smoke and a drink. "Joseph, I remember Mama telling about being sold. She told me slaves treated like cattle. A man went about the country buying up slaves like buying cattle. The man called a 'speculator.' Then he'd sell 'em to the highest bidder. You see children taken from their mother's breast, mothers sold, husbands sold from wives. Then she start singing:

De rough, rocky road what Moses done travel,
I'se bound to carry my soul to de Lord;
It's a mighty rocky road but I must done travel,
And I'se bound to carry my soul to de Lord.

"Then many times Mama, she sing that Sweet Chariot song:

Swing low, sweet chariot
Freely let me into rest,
I don't want to stay here no longer;
Swing low, sweet chariot,
When Gabriel make he last alarm
I wants to be rollin' in Jesus arm,
'Cause I don't want to stay here no longer."

It seemed every time Mary started to talk about slavery, she started singing. "Joseph, my mama a good lady. I hope she is a-walking with the Lord."

"I know she is, Mary."

When Mary and Emma came back from spending the summer with the Power family, Mary Fields wanted to know everything they had done there. Mary told her they had spent the summer taking care of the Powers' child and doing housework. She and Emma did not like the Powers, but it gave them the opportunity to see and remember what it was like to live in a house in the white man's world.

Mary still had a cough from her bout with pneumonia, so when she arrived in Helena Mr. Power took her to the doctor. The doctor told Mary that pneumonia could do permanent damage to the lungs and it would take a long time to get rid of the painful cough.

By the end of the summer, Mary told Miss Fields, she was ready to return to St. Peter's. She had again asked Mr. Power for permission to visit her mother. In a strong, firm voice, he refused, saying it was "impossible"—with no further clarification.

But one day, in Helena, she had met Father Eberschweiler, whom they all knew from St. Peter's Mission. He told her that her mother's health out at the reservation was not good. Mary communicated her concern to him that her mother hadn't been told of Lee Roy's death. Father Eberschweiler went to Mr. Power on their behalf, asking that they be allowed to visit their mother.

Mr. Power conferred with the priest, telling him that it took a long time to get the Indian out of the children, and he did not want them to turn into "wild Indians again." Therefore, they could not have any further contact with their mother.

Father Eberschweiler restated that he had now been transferred from St. Peter's to St. Paul's and that he could supervise any visit by the children. Mr. Power said, "Absolutely not!"

Mary, not knowing that Father Eberschweiler had beseeched Mr. Power on their behalf and feeling desperate to see her mother, went to Mr. Power again. With anger, Mr. Power said that a visit was impossible, and that she should not pursue it again. He stated the reservation was a rough place and that the girls would not be welcome in that world. He claimed that Mary and Emma would be scorned because they were white.

Mary tearfully told Miss Fields how she remembered the wonderful time she had had there with her mother and father, where she was treated neither as an Indian nor as a white—"just a loved person."

She told Mary Fields the Powers did give her a nice sixteenth-birthday party. They gave her a pretty yellow dress and some black patent leather shoes. They also gave Emma a new dress and a pair of pretty shoes.

That evening when Mary Fields saw Joseph, she said, "Joseph, you are good for me, you listen to my anger, you don't tell anyone." She looked at Joseph. "Those Wells children just like slaves, taken from their mother, not allowed to ever see her again, this is wrong. Joseph, this is why I drink and smoke, keep my temper down."

Joseph talked Mary Fields into going to Christmas Eve Mass at 11:30 P.M.

"Why you want me to go to white man's church?"

"For me, Mary."

"For you, Joseph, I will go."

They walked through the cold, clear moonlit night to church. Mother Amadeus lit the new sanctuary lamp that had been sent by Miss Cleve from Boston, for the first time. It sent the most beautiful flickering light throughout the church. All the sisters sang that night to the accompaniment of the violin played by Sister Carmen Dunn.

Mary poked Joseph. "The only reason you come out in this cold is to see that pretty Mary Wells."

"Mary, be quiet, you should be praying."

"I pray, I swear." Joseph had to smile; he had gotten her into the church. Even the nuns were surprised.

At four o'clock the next day all the boys and girls ate dinner, while the sisters provided Christmas music. Mary Wells could see her brother William at the dinner table. He was wearing new pants, a heavy sweater, and boots he had received from Mr. Power. Mary was struck by what a sad and lonesome-looking boy he had become. He missed his brother Lee Roy and didn't seem to want to make a lot of friends. Mary had heard that Joseph Gump was keeping an eye on William at the request of Miss Fields.

Joseph was at dinner, but the girls weren't allowed to talk to the boys or the men. Mary didn't know whether it was her imagination or not, but she felt Mr. Gump's eyes on her. Apparently it wasn't her imagination after all, because later that evening, all the girls teased her about Mr. Gump giving her the eye.

"Not true, not true," Mary said.

Mary Fields got mad at the girls. "You leave that child alone or you deal with me."

Mary asked Miss Fields, "Could such a handsome, good man like me?" She had grown to feel very unsure of herself, especially in the eyes of a white man. She often thought about what a brave and independent man her father must have been to love her Indian mother despite all the obstacles.

CHAPTER SEVENTEEN

Festivals at the Mission

It seemed that the winds were worse that year than most. If the nuns had only known that Mary Fields and Joseph were making bets on how many nuns would fall flat on their backs on the ice each morning on their way to the chapel! Mary was ahead with her guess of four, and in two days in a row four nuns went down. The best day was a Sunday when Father opened the chapel door and the wind swept right through, taking all the vestments, vases, and candlesticks from the altar.

February 7, 1894, was a sad day. At 12:30 A.M., little Lily Cash died from scrofula. They said she was so weak that she died peacefully. Then, at three o'clock the very same morning, Sister Veronica died. She was twenty-two years old and had been a nun for only five months.

The next day a Mass was said, and they were both buried in the new graveyard on a small hill overlooking the mission. A fire was built on the ground to thaw it so that the graves could be dug. Mary Fields and Joseph helped—Mary moved the hot ash as Joseph and other workers dug the graves. They all looked muddy and cold.

On April 20, 1894, everyone at St. Peter's Mission had a big surprise. The old coach, the one on which Mary Fields and many of the children had arrived at the mission, had begun to run again between Fort Benton, Great Falls, and Helena after a long hiatus. Also to everyone's surprise, there were twenty guests—all sisters from other orders who would be doing hospital work in Montana.

Everyone helped Mary Fields prepare food for the mission guests, who were impressed with the meal they received. Sister Joseph of Arimathea, Mother Superior of Fort Benton Hospital, told Mother Amadeus that they wanted to steal Mary Fields. She told Mother Amadeus what a find it was to have her in the middle of Montana. Mother Amadeus replied that the mission could not afford to lose Mary.

It was a busy spring for Mary Fields. On April 29, First Communion was held at the mission for forty-two children. All the girls wore white dresses with veils and flowers studded in their hair; the boys wore white shirts. Mary pressed all the dresses and shirts beforehand, and after communion they had to be washed, pressed, and stored for the next group. The mission always made First Communion Day a very special day with a picnic and games.

The next big day for the mission was May 27, the Feast of Corpus Christi. The sisters had Mary and Joseph plant small trees on both sides of the carriage walk. The two stood back and admired their handiwork as the procession went by. First the cross-bearer, then the girls, the nuns, the boys, the brothers, the choir, and the Blessed Body and Blood of the Lord. The procession went from the cabin past the newly planted trees. Everyone sang hymns along the way:

> Holy, Holy, Holy Lord God of power and might,
> Heaven and earth are full of your glory.
> Hosanna, hosanna in the highest.
> Blessed is he who comes in the name of the Lord.
> Hosanna, hosanna in the highest.

They all felt it was the most beautiful procession the mission had ever held. To Joseph's surprise, Mary slapped him on the back. "Good job, Joseph!" He started to laugh and gave her a small pat on the back. "Good job, Miss Fields!"

Mary and Joseph stood in the back of the church, since it was full, and listened to the priest's sermon about the Feast of Corpus Christi. He started with the Last Supper. The priest said that Jesus was fully aware of the suffering and death that would come to Him the next day when He gathered His disciples at the table this one last time. He embraced everything they were and, indeed, the whole of history, all of human experience. He gathered every part of our lives and brought us all with Him to the Father. He loaded all our sins and all our frailty, and every good thing about us as well, into His own arms and brought it all to His Father. The priest went on to say:

> In the proclamation of St. Mark's Gospel on this Feast of the Body and Blood of Christ, the story is told: Eating, Jesus took a loaf of bread, and after blessing it, gave it to them, and said, "Take; this is My body." Then He took a cup, and after giving thanks He gave it to them and all of them drank from it. He said to them, "This is My blood of the covenant, which is poured out for many." The Letter to the Hebrews comments: "Christ is the mediator of a new covenant, so that those who are called may

receive the promised eternal inheritance, because a death has occurred that redeems them from the transgressions under the first covenant."

After the service, Mary said, "Joseph, after that sermon, how about a drink?"

"Sounds good right now, Mary."

Mary sat back in her chair outside her cabin and lit a cigar. "Joseph, I remember those niggers down on the farms, on most farms, never had a chance to go to Sunday school and church. Yet today was a big day for all them Catholics, the sisters, the brothers and the priests. And I suppose for you and me, Joseph, but I still don't understand. We all equal in the eyes of Jesus and the Father-God, but His representatives sure don't treat us equal—nothing make sense to Mary Fields.

The white folks feared for niggers to get any religion and education, but I reckon something inside just told them about God and that there was a better place hereafter. They sneak off and have prayer meeting. Me, I work for the nuns and not sure there is a God. I got an education, so I can read and write, but not sure there is a God."

"Mary, with what your people went through, I wouldn't be sure of a God either."

The final exams for the year were held on June 25 and 26 for both the white and Indian children. All the students were told that they had done well on the exams and were wished a good summer. Mary Fields would spend the summer preparing the mission for the students' return and another winter.

In the fall Mary was always pleased to see the Wells children return to St. Peter's. Mary Wells gave Miss Fields a big hug. "All right, Mary, tell me about your summer."

Mary told Miss Fields that Mrs. Power had told her she must start thinking about the future; she said Mary could come work as a domestic for them. Mary Fields snorted, "You punch the old lady?"

No, the girl replied, she had just bitten her tongue and said, "Thank you."

Mary Wells went on to tell Miss Fields about her meeting with Senator Power. She had asked him to show her her father's will so she could see what happened to all his money. He told her that he had invested her father's money in more cattle, and they all died in the cold winter of 1886. Mary repeated, "Only the cattle you invested my father's money in died?"

Senator Power said that was right. "I only lost his cattle, so I have been supporting your family with my own money. Besides, my dear, you are still a half-breed and can't own land. You have been well taken care of and have nothing to complain about. Any more questions? If you wish, perhaps you can find your mother and move down to the reservation with her. Would you like that?"

Mary saw his hands start to shake and heard the anger rise in his voice. She read the guilt in this man—his offer for her to return to her mother was a threat, extended only to end the conversation. She knew he would never allow her to join her mother, and he used her most cherished desire to drive home her helplessness. The option to return was not hers. Mary saw that it was useless to ask Senator Power about her father's affairs.

She told Mary Fields she had never been so happy to return to St. Peter's. Mary gave her a big hug. "I know this isn't your real home, but you'll always have a home with me."

September 12 was a big day. Not only was it Mary Wells' seventeenth birthday, but there was to be a wedding at the mission.

Mr. Larry was a local rancher who had given money and time to the mission over the years. While there, he had met Clara Wiegand, who was a student. Having completed her schooling, Clara had returned to her family, who were also ranchers. Clara and Mr. Larry were married in the log cabin church that day. In the morning Mary Wells helped prepare the wedding breakfast for them in the convent.

That afternoon, Miss Fields baked a cake for Mary, and all the Indian children sang to her. Mary had brought a package from Helena, given to her by the Powers, to be opened on her birthday. It was a warm wool sweater. That evening Mary realized that she was the same age as Clara Wiegand, who had been married that very day.

St. Peter's now had nine houses with seventy-four Ursulines; this was considered a big mission.

CHAPTER EIGHTEEN

Joseph Goes Courting

Mary Fields ran to Joseph on a cold December day. "Joseph, you hear what happened?"

"No, Mary, what's going on?"

"You know Mother Amadeus went to Helena to talk to the bishop."

"Yes, so?"

Mary went on to tell Joseph that on the way, the party had crossed Blue Creek, an arm of the Yellowstone. The driver was heading for the new bridge, which had just that day been completed.

Suddenly, the whole party was neck deep in icy water. Large blocks of ice floated down the rapid current. The horses barely kept their lips out of the water. Had the horses moved a step, they would have drowned. Mother Amadeus roused the driver, who had fainted, and instructed him to get to the shore and ride one of the horses to a cowboy shack two miles back. However, the icy jolt made the driver unable to speak when he arrived at the shack. All he finally managed to utter was, "Nuns in the river."

The cowboys rode to the river and managed to save the sisters. It took several hours to get the horses out. The rescuers built a huge fire for the nuns to warm up, but icicles formed on their clothes while they were drying. No one perished or became ill, however.

Mary chuckled, "Joseph, wouldn't you love to see all them nuns in the river with icicles?"

"Mary, you know you're happy no one was hurt?"

"Yeah, Joseph, but every time I get mad at a nun I can yell 'Nuns in the river,' because I may want to put them there."

Joseph just laughed and went back to his work.

When Christmas Eve came, Joseph tried to talk Mary Fields into going to midnight Mass with him again. She said, "I keep telling you, Joseph, only reason you go is to see that Mary Wells, right? You wanna be close to God, you come over after Mass and have a drink with me."

The Christmas midnight Mass was beautiful, as always. The music and voices always sounded better on a cold, crisp night. Mary Fields didn't see Joseph that night, but they did have coffee the next morning.

"Mary, I think—no, I know I am going to court Mary Wells. I saw her last night at midnight Mass, I think I caught her eye. Mary, I want to court her."

"Joseph, you make me happy, I keep telling you she is the girl for you."

"Mary Fields, I thought you were the girl for me?"

"Joseph, this black lady too old for you! When you gonna start courtin?"

"I'll talk to Mother Amadeus tomorrow, when Christmas is over. You know she'll have to talk to Mary Wells."

Joseph told Mother Amadeus about his feelings toward Mary Wells and asked her permission to court the girl. Mother Amadeus said she would talk to Mary and let him know.

When Joseph saw Mary Fields that evening, she was smiling. "Joseph, Mother Amadeus must have talked to Mary Wells. The word is all over the school Joseph wants to court her." Joseph started to blush. "Joseph, I never seen you blush before!" She told him that there were going to be a lot of jealous girls at the school.

Mother Amadeus told Joseph that it had been arranged for him to meet Mary Wells at the convent on Sunday afternoon, January 13, 1895. The first meeting would be in the convent parlor, and their chaperone would be Sister Marguerite.

Mary sat next to Joseph, who told her about himself, as he had told Mary Fields before. Whenever Mary spoke, he seemed to cherish everything about her. His look stirred a memory of her own father looking at her lovingly when she was a child.

Miss Fields interrupted with a pot of tea, grinning at them. "Can I get you children anything else?"

Joseph gave her a half-smile. "No, thank you, Miss Fields."

"Mr. Gump," Mary Wells said.

"Please, Mary, call me Joseph, or Joe."

Mary replied, "Yes, sir," then wanted to disappear under the sofa. She had grown accustomed a long time ago to address all white men as "sir." "I mean, yes, Joseph." He smiled warmly at her.

Mary and Joseph agreed to meet again the following Sunday at the convent, which really was the only meeting place available in the winter. This time, in front of Sister Marguerite,

Joseph took Mary's hand and kissed it when he said good-bye. Mary felt as if she would faint.

When Joseph left that day, Sister Marguerite said, "He sure is a good-looking man." Mary thought it was funny to hear a sister say something like that. "Yes, he sure is," she replied.

As she walked into the Indian girls' log cabin, she was greeted with dozens of questions. "Is he nice?" "Do you like him?" "Are you going to see him again?" and on and on.

Mary looked forward to their next Sunday meeting and to learning more about him. She was almost afraid to speak of her own life, for some reason. But it seemed that Joseph was already well informed about her through Miss Fields.

Mother Amadeus called a meeting of the sisters and Mary Fields about the boarding school. It seemed they were always being hit by an epidemic, either of tuberculosis, trachoma, measles, pneumonia, mumps, or just plain influenza, all of which regularly swept through the overcrowded dormitories. They must find a way to stop these epidemics. Mary told Mother Amadeus that they needed more warm clothes and warm bedding, and all the dormitories must be kept cleaner.

The very next morning Theresa Lewis died of pneumonia. She was only fifteen years old.

The following day Theresa was brought to the chapel in a coffin built at the mission. Mother Amadeus, the sisters, and all the children met the coffin at the door. Theresa's remains were followed by her mother, father, and sisters. Father Rebman, who had the most beautiful voice Mary had ever heard, sang the Mass of the Angels. The funeral service was conducted by Father Schuyler.

Mary Fields did attend and sat with Mary and Joseph. After the service Mary Wells said to Miss Fields that if she died, neither her father nor her mother would be there, and most likely her mother wouldn't even be told. She said that she thought she would like to be buried at the mission when she died, next to her brother.

Mary said that when she had started to cry during the funeral, Joseph had reached down and taken her hand. His hand was so rough and strong. She told Miss Fields how good it felt. Miss Fields smiled. "I saw him take your hand, old Mary don't miss much."

Mary Wells' bad cough returned that winter, and Dr. Adams from Great Falls saw her on one of his visits to the mission. He told her that her congested chest would come and go for the rest of her life; she must always be wary of catching pneumonia again, as the next time it could be fatal. "I must have my father's lungs," Mary told him, remembering her father's terrible coughing spells.

Mary Fields asked Dr. Adams if there was anything special she could do for the children. He told her he thought she was doing a lot, and without her the mission would have much more sickness.

On March 7 the mission was to celebrate the anniversary of the arrival of its first Indian pupils. One of the first eleven Blackfoot girls, Rosada, had been just a baby then and was still at the mission. Mary Fields asked Mother Amadeus why the Wells girls weren't counted anywhere.

She gave the same story, that Mary and Emma weren't counted because they were Gros Ventres (A'aninin) and had been sent there by Senator Power. The mission had very few Gros Ventres. Besides, she said, Mary and Emma had their board and care paid for. Then, Mary asked, why were they put with the other Indians and not with the white students? Mother Amadeus became impatient. "Mary, they are Indians."

"Yes, Dolly." Mary would call Mother Amadeus that when she was mad. "That's why the sisters call them the 'very white Indians.'" With that last remark she walked out. Mother Amadeus just shook her head. "That Mary Fields."

On March 29, Mother Amadeus' feast day, Mary Fields made refreshments for the fathers and the boys; each received a small cake, a ball of popcorn, an orange, a hot roll, and a ball of butter. Mother Amadeus was given a beautiful bookcase that the brothers and Joseph had made. The bookcase was placed in the parlor of the convent, which would eventually become the library.

Joseph told Mary Fields he was going to ask Mary Wells to marry him on Easter Sunday. He knew he would have to leave his job at St. Peter's, because there was no housing there for married workers; all the men lived with the Jesuit brothers. Joseph really didn't want to leave, but marrying Mary was more important to him. He had begun to look for other work and had just been offered a job as foreman in the lead mines in Marysville, Montana. Mary told Joseph it was time for him to move on.

Easter Sunday arrived, April 14, with a heavy snowstorm descending. There was still a celebration at the mission. Mary Wells met Joseph at three o'clock that afternoon in the parlor. Joseph seemed nervous. Many families were coming in and out that day, and the novices entertained everyone with music and elocution. It was hard for Mary and Joseph to have any privacy.

Finally, Joseph took Mary by the hand and drew her over to a corner, next to the new bookcase. Taking both of her hands in his, he looked into her eyes. "Mary, will you please marry me?

I love you and have loved you from the first time I saw you in the window."

Mary wanted this more than anything. She felt the veil that had surrounded her since her father died begin to part. She replied, "Yes, Joseph, I will."

Joseph told her that he would talk to Mother Amadeus and would also let the mines in Marysville know that he would be coming by early fall. He suggested they plan on July for their wedding. Mary agreed that July wasn't too soon.

Mary was the happiest she had ever been in her life. She told Joseph that she would only tell Mary Fields, because if she told Emma, who was such a gossip, it would be all over the mission.

In May, Dodie Sanborn, a Gros Ventre girl, came down with an acute case of erysipelas, an infectious skin inflammation accompanied by fever. She was isolated so that the infection wouldn't spread among the others at the mission. No one knew where the infection had come from. The sisters sent for Dr. Adams, who immediately took Dodie to Great Falls.

Mother Amadeus gave the other Gros Ventre girls permission to travel to Great Falls to see Dodie, who had been kept in the hospital there. She asked one of the men working at the mission to go with them as a guide. (Usually, Joseph would have been asked, but he was in Helena buying supplies.) All the workmen at the mission refused to accompany the girls to Great Falls, saying they didn't wish to travel with half-breeds and Indians. Mother Amadeus was shocked and furious to think that Christian men at the mission could hold that attitude. The girls heard about it, and it only reminded them that this attitude was everywhere in the outside world and they were just sheltered from it at the mission.

Mary despaired, wondering if perhaps Joseph, because he had been born in Germany, somehow didn't even know she was half-Indian. But of course he did.

Mary Fields said she would take the girls to Great Falls. It was fun for them being on their own, singing tribal songs, and not a white around to look down on them. They stayed a week at the convent in Great Falls while visiting Dodie, who was very happy to see her friends and appeared to be recovering. It was a wonderful trip.

CHAPTER NINETEEN

Gunfight at the Mission

During the latter part of May, a terrible thing happened at the mission. Joseph had gone to Cascade for supplies, and Mary Fields was acting as foreman for both the girls' school and the boys' school. One of the workers did not take kindly to having a black woman tell him what to do.

Mary tried to give the man orders, but he wouldn't pay any attention to her. She gave him a direct order, and he barked back that "no white man should take orders from a nigger slave."

Mary very politely told the worker that there weren't any slaves at the mission and to please get back to work. The fellow walked right up to her, swung at her and knocked her down, while some of the other men started to laugh.

All two hundred and more pounds of Mary Fields got to her feet and told the man to get his six-shooter and meet her out in back of the barn.

The nuns couldn't believe what was happening, nor could they stop it. Mary went to her room, stuck her six-shooter in her belt, and headed for the back side of the barn. The man showed up with his gun strapped on. All the workers had gathered to watch the gunfight and many were making bets.

Mary looked the man right in the eyes. "It's your move first." He drew first, but she was faster, and she put two fatal shots into him.

Mary put her gun back into her belt and yelled, "Now let's all get back to work, or there will be more than one funeral at the mission."

Everyone was amazed; they had all thought Mary would be the one to be killed. Mary yelled at them all to leave the dead man lying where he fell. Then she walked over to the barnyard and started doing her work.

When Joseph arrived, Mother Amadeus met him and told him what had happened. He walked out and told two men to bury the dead man. Mother Amadeus asked Joseph if he shouldn't have a church service. Joseph said, "No, just bury him."

Joseph found Mary in front of her cabin. "Mary, what happened?"

"That man hit me. No man ever hit Mary Fields."

"Mary, you must have been real mad?"

"Yes, I was mad. It was like all the times anybody treat me bad all come up together at once.

"Joseph, you shoulda seen the surprised look on that man's face. I swear he could see that bullet coming to him. He knew he was dead."

"This thing will blow over in a couple of days, Mary; no one's going to challenge you again." He gave her a big hug. "Mary, I'm going to always keep you on my side." Joseph had a big smile on his face.

Within a week, the story was all over the territory—a black woman shooting a white man in a gunfight. The bishop was very upset that this had happened at his mission. He sent word to Mother Amadeus that Mary Fields must go.

Joseph wrote to Bishop Brondel telling him the shooting was justified. Mother Amadeus told the bishop it was a mistake to make Mary leave. But he wouldn't change his mind.

Everyone was going to Mother Amadeus and Joseph, hoping the story wasn't true and that Mary wouldn't be leaving. When word went through the mission that Miss Fields must leave, it broke Mary Wells' heart.

She ran to Miss Fields, hoping that the story wasn't true. When she found out it was, she started to cry. The more Miss Fields held her, the harder Mary cried. Mary wanted to leave the mission with her.

No one could change Joseph's mind; he knew that Mary Fields was getting a bad deal. She was a real asset to the mission, and her leaving was a great loss. And the bishop would learn what a mistake it was. In fact, the bishop felt Mary had been a problem from the first day she arrived, and the shooting was a culmination of this in his mind.

CHAPTER TWENTY

Mary Says Good-bye

Mother Amadeus knew everyone in the Cascade area; she sent Mary Fields into town to apply for a job as a driver for Wells Fargo and Company, delivering United States Mail under contract. Mary went into the Wells Fargo and Company office and asked to see the man who was doing the hiring. She told him she wanted a job.

He told her they didn't hire women, especially black women. She said, "I'm Mary Fields—Black Mary. I can outshoot, outride any man trying for this job, you don't want to try me?"

"Sorry, lady, fill out this. You that friend of Mother Amadeus's?"

"Yes."

"You come back tomorrow."

Mary went to the saloon and got a room for that night. She put her bag in the room and went down to get a drink, always carrying her shotgun. She went up to the bar. "Whiskey, and don't tell me ladies don't drink here or my shotgun might go off."

The bartender looked at her. "You Black Mary?"

"I sure is."

"Your drink is on the house."

"Thank you."

She turned. "Anyone play cards?"

A man at the far table put his hand up. "You want to play, Mary?"

Mary went over, set her drink down, and put her hand out. "I'm Mary."

The man pushed his hat back. "I'm Bill, Bill Jackson," he said as he shook her hand. "It seems you got most the people in here afraid of you."

"I like to keep it that way."

The two of them played cards for a couple of hours. When Mary said she wanted to call it a night, they checked their chips and Mary was ahead only a couple of dollars. She put out her hand. "Maybe I will see you again."

The next morning she went to the office. "Mr. Moran here?"

A clerk ran to get him. "Well, Miss Fields, it looks like you got the job, you scared everyone else off."

She would be driving a mail coach around the surrounding area. One of her routes would be the Mullan Road that went past St. Peter's Mission. Mary said she knew that route; the upper part of it would be tough, as it went through some badlands occupied by many outlaws.

Mary told Mr. Moran she had to return the wagon to the mission and get her things and would be ready for work in a couple of days. That was fine with him.

On the way back Mary was sad; she would be leaving her friends at the mission. She told everyone that she would be

Mary Says Good-bye

delivering the mail and supplies to the mission. Mary packed all her things in a wagon so Joseph could drive her back to Cascade. She told Mary Wells she would be at her wedding—no matter what came up, she would be there.

On the way back to Cascade, Mary started to talk. She said she felt like a slave again, because Bishop Brondel with a wave of his hand could send her away from her friends and family.

"That Bishop Brondel like old slaveholder. He separates me from my family. That was all part of slavery, you sell, trade, transfer, auction. Mothers taken from children, wives from husbands, children from parents, fathers from sons and daughters, and brothers and sisters from one another. My only family Mother Amadeus and the mission. That slaveholder everyone bows to is the master."

"Mary, you must move on. You have family, you have Mary and me."

"Joseph, everyone is afraid of me and I'm going to keep it that way."

Mary had taken a permanent room over the saloon. Joseph helped her move in. "Joseph, I want you to come downstairs and watch me."

They went into the saloon and walked up to the bar. "Two whiskeys, please."

"See, Joseph, I'm the only lady in Montana can drink in a bar, not only drink but live in it. Now watch this. Bartender!"

"Yes, miss?"

"What my name?"

"You're Mary, the black coach driver."

Joseph started to laugh. "Mary, you will own Cascade in a couple of weeks."

Joseph had to start back for the mission; he told Mary he would see her when she delivered the mail.

Mary went over to the Wells Fargo and Company office and told them she would be ready for work the next morning. Then she went into the saloon, ordered a steak dinner, found Mr. Jackson for a couple of games of cards, said good-night and went up to her room. She felt if she could keep the fear around her she would be safe out on her route.

It was hard being away from the mission. She could feel tears in her eyes for the first time in years. She said to herself, "Black Mary, you too tough to cry." But in truth she wasn't; she was a very soft, loving person who had just lost her whole family. She thought to herself again, "That Bishop Brondel make a great slavemaster."

Mary could remember her mother telling her how painful it was being separated from her husband and how the slave trade wreaked havoc with slave families. The sale of individual slaves away from parents, children, and loved ones occurred regularly everywhere in the slave-holding South. It kept going through her mind over and over. She was free, yet she was "the bishop's slave."

"You dismissed and sent away from your family, Mary Fields," or he probably called her "Black Mary." She knew he wasn't colorblind. He had never liked her, but of course she didn't like him either. But he had won in the end.

Mary was at the mail office early the next morning. The company she would be working for had once carried passengers, express, mail, treasure, and freight between Helena, Virginia City, and Salt Lake City. From Helena, stages had gone north along the Missouri River to Fort Benton, where the passengers would travel by steamboat to Omaha and St. Louis, avoiding the dangerous overland route east from Salt Lake City.

Mary Says Good-bye

With the advance of railroads into Montana, the stagecoach business started to fall off. But Wells, Fargo and Company found that by using other stagecoach companies and the railroad, their firm could accomplish what it had always done in banking and acting as a forwarding agent for both express and treasure.

Wells, Fargo and Company also still had contracts to deliver the United States Mail, which were very lucrative for them. They paid their drivers well, and the jobs were highly sought after. Mary knew she was very lucky to have a job with them.

Mr. Moran had her route laid out. She was to go to Great Falls and Fort Benton and back, and she should be able to do it in one day. Her wagon was all hitched up for her, but she still checked all of her equipment herself. She said to the man from the stable, "Don't want anything to fall apart on me."

All the mailbags and supplies were marked with where she was to drop them off. She got on her wagon, put her shotgun next to her, and checked her six-shooter in her waistband. It would be an easy trip with not much mud, since the ground was still frozen.

Mary remembered when, in November, she had gotten lost halfway between the mission and Cascade and had to spend the night on the trail. She was sure happy she had her buckskin and buffalo coat. She had to walk all night to keep from freezing. Everyone at the mission thought she was dead. She told Joseph, "Take more than a snowdrift to kill me."

Mary was smiling: she sure would miss Joseph, especially the times when they would have their whiskey and talk.

Mary Fields had promised Mary Wells she would come to the mission for her confirmation on June 29. It was going to be hard, since the bishop would be there and she would have to keep her big mouth shut, if only for Mary's sake.

On June 8 a big snowstorm hit the area and left four feet of snow in Cascade. Mary thought there would be more snow than that at the mission, and it would probably kill the gardens. But that did not stop her from keeping her promise. Mary's boss let her use the company wagon since she would be delivering the mail to the mission. She got her best buckskin out for the trip.

She arrived at the mission on June 28. Everyone was so happy to see her; she was given her old cabin, which was clean with fresh bedding. As soon as she was settled Mary Wells showed up at her door. "Oh, Miss Fields, you are here for my confirmation, thank you."

"Do you think I would miss this day?"

Mary kept on hugging Miss Fields. "I miss you so much."

"I miss you too, Mary."

Mary Wells had to go and help prepare for the next day. Miss Fields pulled her old chair out and was leaning back against the wall when Joseph came over. "Mary, I have never seen you so relaxed. Did you see what a mess your garden is in?"

"Yes, Joseph, and the hens looked like they ready to die, but I don't care. Joseph, got me a bottle whiskey in my room, you want a drink?"

"With you, Mary, anytime."

Mary went in and got the bottle and a couple of small glasses. Her glass of whiskey got her thinking about the old days on the farm. She told Joseph that the slaves used whiskey, rum, beer, wine, or any other alcohol they could get out of frustration. It was a way to get away from the real world. The old planters and farmers tried hard to get the liquor away from the slaves, but they would find it, it was available, and "Joseph, they used it."

"Mary, maybe you should have a couple of shots before you see the bishop tomorrow?"

"You afraid I shoot the bishop tomorrow?"

"Yes, Mary, I am."

Mary had dinner with the sisters and Mother Amadeus, who had a hundred questions for her about her job and new life. Mother Amadeus told Mary the garden was a mess and the chickens weren't laying; Mary was sorely needed at the mission. Mary just listened, making sure Mother Amadeus didn't know how much she also missed all of them.

Mary Wells came over to Miss Fields to tell her all that was going on. Her first banns of marriage would be announced on July 6, 1895, at Mass.

Mary Fields took her hand. "I'm so proud of you and Joseph."

"Are you going to be at our wedding?"

"I'll be there no matter what, unless some bandit shoots me."

"Mary, please don't say things like that. Both you and I have lost many people in our lives."

"I'm sorry, Mary, I shouldn't joke like that."

The next day was busy for the mission; Mary Fields enjoyed watching all the activity and just being a guest. At eleven o'clock everyone went to the church for the Mass said by the bishop. Halfway through the Mass he confirmed both adults and children from around the area, and twenty-six girls from the mission school.

Joseph was sitting with Mary Fields. She poked him. "That Mary Wells sure a beauty."

She could see Joseph turn red. "Yes, she is."

That afternoon after lunch the bishop toured the mission. He visited the Indian girls' new, not-yet-finished log cabin and blessed it. It seemed to everyone that the bishop and Mary

Fields were trying to avoid each other. Joseph stayed at her side and kept talking to her to keep her calm.

Mary said good-bye to everyone and told them she had to be back in Cascade for a mail run the next morning. Mother Amadeus told her again how much they missed her. Mary just couldn't hold back any longer. "You tell that slavemaster bishop that."

Mother Amadeus took her hand. "Mary, we must do God's will. The bishop is the church's representative, and I must follow his orders."

"Mother Amadeus, you know I love you, and you know he is your boss, but not mine."

Mary Wells and Joseph were the last to say good-bye. Mary Fields was happy to have seen her friends again, but the trip back to Cascade was lonely. She kept thinking about Mary Wells just wanting to find her mother. She remembered slave children running away, trying to find their mothers. The chances of success were very remote; the children usually wandered in vain until they were caught and returned to their owners. The Indian children got caught and returned to the mission; it was exactly the same.

Mary's mail route took her to St. Peter's Mission about once a week, and she would stop for an hour or so each time. Mary Wells told her that the wedding date had been set for July 23 at ten o'clock Mass and that she must be there. She promised Mary again that she would. Mary wrote a note telling her that the second banns of marriage had been announced on July 13.

She told Miss Fields that as the day grew closer, she was realizing that she would soon be leaving the mission, where she had spent much of her life. She would also be leaving behind her closest friend, as well as her sister and brother, for whom her mother had asked her to care. It was Mary's full intent to have Emma come to live with her as soon as Emma completed her schooling.

There would be so many changes for Mary. She would be alone with Joseph Gump all the time, and what would that be like? Though she was excited, she was also very frightened. Why, in gaining something so wonderful, did she have to lose so much?

She finished the letter telling her friend how she was looking forward to having her at her wedding. Mary Fields put the letter down. "That girl growing up, she is ready to get married."

She looked at the envelope; it read:

Miss Mary Fields
The Saloon
Cascade, Montana

She chuckled. "That one damn good address—The Saloon."

CHAPTER TWENTY-ONE

The Wedding of Mary and Joseph

Mary Fields got permission again to use the mail wagon and keep it at the mission overnight. When she arrived on July 22 she was given her old room, and again it was clean with clean bedding. She found Joseph. "You look scared, Joseph, wanna take a walk around the mission?" He readily agreed.

"You know, Joseph, the thing I miss most is my garden and hennery. Can't have 'em at the saloon. I wanna find a house, no one wants Black Mary around. Joseph, they still have that old eagle I shot?"

"Yes, and they will probably give him to you tomorrow, since Mary and I will be leaving."

"I guess he can ride in the wagon on my mail route."

Joseph told Mary that they had planted a garden, but there had been an invasion of potato bugs. The weeds and bugs had gotten ahead of those who were taking care of the fields. The whole mission was out killing potato bugs and weeding the fields—priests, sisters, boy and girl students. "Mary, it took the whole mission to do the work you did alone, and they still lost most of the garden."

Mary looked at Joseph. "I'm gone, and next you. What this mission gonna do?"

"They pray a lot, and things will work out."

"Joseph, you take care o' that Mary. You always be a family. I told you there wasn't any marrying on the farm when I was young. Women raised all their own children, like my mama. Never knew who my papa was. Mary lose both her papa and mama. You know you must always be family, or Joseph, I shoot you."

"I will take care of Mary always, or you can shoot me."

The two friends sat back in two chairs in front of Mary's old cabin and had a smoke and a little whiskey. "Mary, you don't have any trouble drinking in the saloon in Cascade?"

"Joseph, who gonna question me?" Joseph smiled, sat back and closed his eyes; he had a wonderful friend sitting next to him.

Mary Wells woke early on July 23, 1895. Mother Elizabeth helped her get ready. Many of the sisters buzzed about Mary and Emma, working on their hair and helping them into their dresses. At last, Mother Elizabeth told Mary to look at herself in the mirror. The bride turned and saw a beautiful young woman, with long, shiny black hair that her mother would have been proud of, ready to start her new life. She wished her mother could be there.

Miss Fields went over to Mary's room to see if she could help. She had on a new buckskin outfit she had made just for this special day. Mary Wells grabbed her, giving her a big hug. "Thank you for being here for me." Miss Fields stood back.

The Wedding of Mary and Joseph

"Mary, I wouldn't miss this show for anything. You look beautiful. I'm even going into the chapel."

"You certainly are," said Mary, "and you'll be sitting in the front row to act as my mother."

As she entered the chapel, Mary realized that it was completely full, but she kept her eyes straight ahead. She had her brother William walk her down the aisle, since her father was no longer alive and she refused to have T. C. Power do it. That man could never stand in for her father; she didn't even like him.

The beauty of the organ music and the angelic singing of nuns and children absorbed Mary Fields' thoughts. Both William and Joseph looked so handsome in their new suits. Mary could see how nervous everyone was, especially Joseph, who was shaking. But the wedding Mass was beautiful, and she did feel like the bride's mother.

As always at the mission, there had to be some excitement. Just as they were leaving the church at the close of the ceremony, a fire broke out in the wash house. Some blankets near the chimney in the upper room were found smoldering. But the fire was put out very quickly by the brothers, who wouldn't let Joseph help fight in his new suit. Miss Fields just watched and wouldn't lend a hand.

At the wedding breakfast Mary Fields sat with Father Prando, who had performed the ceremony. He thought she still worked at the mission and kept asking her questions. She finally said to him, "Father, I was fired by the bishop for killing a worker who asked too many questions." He didn't ask her another question that whole breakfast.

Mary asked William how he liked his work at Fort Benton for T. C. Power and whether he was being treated well. He told her that things were all right; he was an accountant and had a room in the warm house, so he was like a guard at night.

To Mary Fields, Emma looked so grown-up in her special dress. Seeing her laughing from across the room, Mary knew it wouldn't be long before Emma was ready to marry. A photographer from Great Falls took the wedding pictures. The nuns had brought him to the mission as a wedding present to Mary Wells.

At noon, Joseph brought his wagon around, and the bride changed into her favorite blue dress. She gave her wedding dress to the sisters so that someone else might use it.

Over the past few days Mary had been packing up the few things she had, remembering to take her silver from its hiding place in the wall. Now these were placed into Joseph's wagon. Everyone was hugging Mary, and many of the sisters cried, though Mary couldn't imagine that it would be long before she would be back for a visit.

She gave her last big hug to all the nuns, her little sister Emma, and Miss Fields. She told them each how much she loved them, and made Miss Fields promise to come to Marysville for a visit.

Mary Fields spent a couple more hours visiting with the girls and nuns, but she wanted to get back to Cascade before dark. The last thing she did was to catch her eagle, put a strap on its leg, and tie it to the wagon seat. As she left the mission, she could feel everyone's eyes on her—Black Mary, with an eagle sitting next to her.

Chapter Twenty-Two

Driving with the Bird

When Mary got back to Cascade, she put up her horse and wagon and went into the saloon with the eagle on her arm. The bartender looked at her. "Mary, what you got there?"

"This here is my roommate, only man getting in there. Two whiskeys—one for me, one for my man."

It was a sight to see. The eagle would dip its beak in the whiskey, tilt its head back and swallow, then shake its head back and forth very fast. It would look at Mary and then do the whole act again. Mary had a new drinking partner.

When she left on her route the next morning, the eagle was sitting on the wagon seat next to her. She knew she would have to start shooting game to feed her eagle. The eagle was a great attraction at each stop, but people had to stay away from it or it would bite them. Mary would laugh when it got a finger and drew blood. She would say over and over, "My partner bites."

She ran into one man who threatened to kill her eagle after it bit him. Mary stood up with her pistol exposed in her belt. "You come across me to get to my bird."

He looked at her for a minute, then said, "Ah, that damn bird ain't worth me killing you to get at."

The bartender told the man he was lucky—Black Mary was fast and had killed many a man. The man kept looking at Mary from across the room. Mary didn't like his looks; she said, "Buster, you stop looking this way or I will take your eyes." He left the saloon.

"That man won't stop until he get to California," the bartender said.

Mary got up. "Got an early run. You make everyone around afraid of me."

"Hell, Mary, I would not fight you. Even some parents use you to scare their children—'If you're not good, I'll give you to Black Mary.'"

Mary said, "That true?"

"Oh, yes, I hear them talk."

Mary took her eagle and went up to her room.

The trips became routine for Mary; the main thing she could boast of was that no bandits had hit her wagon. On one of her trips to St. Peter's Mission she could see that there had been an early frost; it was only September, and the potatoes had frozen. They were trying to harvest them, but Mary told them they would only rot. It was hard on the mission, since they depended on this crop.

Mary could remember harvesting the potatoes and storing them in a dry dark place in the straw. They would last until spring, and the ones that sprouted were cut up for planting a new crop. She really had enjoyed working in the garden.

Mother Amadeus passed through Cascade on her way to Great Falls on September 7. She found Mary at the saloon. Mary invited Mother Amadeus into her "home." The nun sat very flustered at Mary's table in the corner.

Mary was enjoying seeing Mother Amadeus this way. Mary had full power in this environment. They made quite a sight—a nun, an eagle, and a black woman sitting in a saloon.

"Mother Amadeus, you want a sarsaparilla? Bartender, a sarsaparilla for the sister and two whiskeys, one for me and one for the eagle."

Mother Amadeus had a two-hour wait for her stage. The longer the two sat talking about the farm in Tennessee, the more Mother Amadeus became relaxed. She even started to laugh as the eagle drank the whiskey.

Mary walked Mother Amadeus out to her stage. The two hugged and said, "We will always be good friends!"

Mary Wells Gump was good about writing to Mary Fields, and she would save each letter. The first one she received told about their house and what a shack it was—a small, two-bedroom house that was an awful mess. Mary said it looked as though pigs had lived in it. There was mud, rotten food, garbage, and dirty wood for the stove scattered all across the floors. The walls were streaked with dirt. She and Joseph had to sleep in the wagon until they could clean and paint the place.

Mary was anxious to go to Marysville to see the Gumps. She wrote to Mary to tell her she would try to see Emma on each trip to the mission. Emma was looking forward to spending time next summer in Marysville with them. She was doing well, but was ready to leave the mission.

Mary Gump wrote back to Miss Fields, thanking her for keeping an eye on Emma, and telling her more about

Marysville. From her porch there, Mary could see two small white churches, side by side, one Catholic and one Protestant. With all the Irish living in the area, she figured that the Catholic church would fill faster, but she soon learned that there were both Northern and Southern Irish living there and that they didn't mix well.

She told Mary Fields she would fit well in Marysville, because they had a tradition that Joseph learned the first day. As soon as their shift ended, the miners all went to the saloon for shots of whiskey and ale. But of course, Joseph would only have one, then tell everyone he was newly married and wanted to go home.

Mary wrote that the men worked in the mines six days a week, ten hours a day. Joseph was tired, but still made their house the most beautiful on the hill. Mary Fields would smile; it was good knowing Mary was happy. She only wished she could be as happy; it was lonesome for her in Cascade.

When the weather got cold Mary's trips were limited, so she spent more time in the saloon playing cards. It was good, since in actuality she was making more money at the card table than she did driving the mail wagon. The old eagle was always on the chair next to her. Some of the other card players would accuse Mary of having the eagle look at their cards and tell her what they had. Many of the other players would buy her eagle a drink of whiskey just to see it go through the act. After a couple of drinks it would just go to sleep.

Mary got a chance to take a load of freight to Fort Belknap. It was a long, cold trip. She kept thinking it was about time to move back to Tennessee, where she could at least be warm.

From Fort Belknap Mary went down to St. Paul's Mission to see Father Malkin and spend the night with the Ursuline sisters from St. Peter's, Mother Francis and Sister Martha. Mary was welcome, and the evening was spent talking about St. Peter's Mission. The Ursulines were surprised to see that Mary had the eagle with her. Sister Martha found some raw chicken to feed it. Mary thought to herself, all that bird needed was the same thing she needed—a good shot of whiskey.

The next day the nuns showed Mary the school, where they had over 160 Indian children, all from the reservation. Mary couldn't understand why the Powers wouldn't let the Wells children come back to St. Paul's. It was a nice, well-run school.

The nuns told Mary that the Gumps had come through the mission on their way to Marysville, and how hard it had been on Mary to find out that her mother had died the year before. Mary Fields could feel the anger inside herself, wondering why small children had to be taken from family the way they were.

By mid-morning she was back on the trail with a basket of food that would last her all the way back to Cascade. She went as far as Havre for the first night. The room she found was dirty, but there wasn't any other available. She was pleased to have the food the Ursulines had made for her, with the special packages for her eagle.

Mary got the same question from everyone: "You got a name for that bird?"

"No," she would always answer, "just 'Bird'." She couldn't understand why she kept him, but she could hear Mary Wells saying, "You can't kill an eagle, it is very bad luck." But that eagle sure killed her chickens. She had to laugh, thinking about that Mary Wells standing up for that dumb eagle.

Mary spent the next night in Fort Benton; she wanted to stop and see how William was doing at his job and whether Power was treating him with respect. She found Willie at his accounting job. He was a very lonely-looking young man. He told Mary he had a girlfriend named Flora who was white and didn't care if he was half-breed. Mary told Willie that she and his sister were corresponding. Willie knew this, since he and his sister were writing to each other also.

Mary left Willie and went down to the Grand Union Hotel, which was located right on the Missouri River. The desk clerk didn't know how to take Mary. He had seen many frontier men, but never anything like this short, heavy black woman dressed in buckskin and a buffalo coat, with an eagle on one arm and a shotgun on the other.

The hotel was a little run-down, but was still one of the fanciest Mary had stayed in. She said to the clerk, "I need a room for the night—with a bath."

"Oh, yes, please sign here."

Mary looked at the book, took the pen, and wrote, "Black Mary. Cascade."

"Oh, Miss Black Mary, that will be a dollar twenty-five for the room and twenty-five cents for a bath. So a dollar fifty in advance."

Mary paid and he gave her a key. "Room 203, that's on the second floor." Mary smiled, took her small bag and shotgun in one hand, and headed for the stairs.

The room overlooked the Missouri, which was frozen. There was a knock on the door; when Mary answered, there stood a small Indian girl with two buckets of hot water. She didn't say a word, but walked over to the tin tub and poured the water in. She slipped out as quietly as she had come in.

Mary checked the water, took off her clothes, lit a cigar, and got into the tub. The water was a little hot, but it felt good all over her body. She was 64 years old, still working hard. She wondered how much longer she could last.

After her bath she went down to the saloon and ordered a steak dinner and a whiskey. Just as she was relaxing with her dinner, a very old man came over and stuck out his hand. "I'm Jake, and you that famous Black Mary. I always wanted to meet you, can I sit down?"

Mary looked at him and wondered if she looked that old. "Jake, can I buy you a whiskey?"

"Oh no, Miss Black Mary, I can buy my own. You know you are the only woman in this saloon?"

"Yes, I know, it's that way most of the time."

He started to tell her about the hotel. It had been finished in 1882. All the interior moldings were made by hand, using wooden planes; he knew this because he had been one of the carpenters. He told her that the hotel had a saddle room where cowboys stored their saddles for the winter, and a very fancy dining room that she should see.

He pointed upward and told her the first floor had a secret lookout room where guards watched gold shipments. Mary had to laugh when he told her about the "ladies' stairs," which led to elegant parlors above, for ladies never entered rooms adjoining saloons at any time.

He wanted her to note that each room was heated by its own wood stove and had its own fancy chimney. All Mary could think about was all the chimney fires they had at the mission.

Old Jake went on about this Grand Union Hotel. He didn't seem to want anything except to have someone listen to him and to be around the famous Black Mary. Mary was tired; soon she excused herself and went back to her room. Her talk with Jake did make her take another look at her room. The furnishings were all black walnut with marble tops—the same kind of furnishings she had had in the big house back at the farm.

The last thing Jake had told Mary was that the Grand Union was there to welcome weary travelers to spend a few nights in its luxury before they set out to less civilized places, such as Virginia City, Helena, Missoula, Idaho, and points west of the Mullan Road. Mary smiled to herself—less civilized places such as Cascade and St. Peter's Mission.

Mary got up early, hitched up her wagon, and was on the trail to Cascade on a fine Montana morning. It had been a pleasant night in a fancy hotel. She looked at her eagle. "You old eagle in fancy hotels."

It was cold. Mary's mind went back to the farm and going to church. She could heard her mother saying, "All de niggers love to go to church, and sing."

> I wanna be ready
> I wanna be ready
> I wanna be ready, good Lord
> To walk in Jerusalem
> Just like John
> John say de city was just four square.
> To walk in Jerusalem just like John
> But I'll meet my mother and father there,
> To walk in Jerusalem, just like John.

Mary found herself singing out loud with not a soul to hear but her old eagle. It would have been wonderful to go to old Jerusalem and see her father and mother.

Mary was happy to get back to her room in Cascade. The weather was changing and becoming very cold. It looked like she wouldn't be going out for a while.

CHAPTER TWENTY-THREE

A Trip to Tennessee

IT WAS GETTING COLDER EACH DAY. Mary went to her boss and asked for some time off to go to Tennessee. She would take a stage to Havre, where she could catch a train to Tennessee.

She went to the saloon and paid for her room for the next four months, then wrote notes to Mary Gump and Mother Amadeus telling them where she would be. She could catch a stage the next day for Havre. Mary was packed and ready when the stage arrived. It was empty except for her and her eagle going north. The stage trip took two days, with the usual stops in Great Falls and Fort Benton.

In Havre she had to wait a day for the train going east. This would be Mary's first train ride. The trip would take about a week, with changes in St. Paul, Chicago, and Indianapolis. From Louisville she would take a stage to the farm.

Mary wasn't much of an attraction in Montana and the Dakota area, but as the train started south she would turn heads when she went to the dining car in her buckskins, with an eagle on her arm and her shotgun at her side.

As the train passed Chicago, all the black people were put in separate train cars. Mary would talk to some of the black folks, who told her things were hard for them in the South, but not as hard as in slave times. An old woman looked at Mary. "You wear crazy clothes and got one funny bird, but you musta been a slave." Mary told her she had been a slave on a farm in Tennessee, but now lived in Montana. The old woman wanted to know where Montana was and if they had niggers there. Mary told her no, but it wasn't easy for her, and her name was Black Mary. The old woman would just go on talking.

"You know, Mary, a lot of de niggers in slavery time worked so hard dey said dey hated to see de sun rise in de morning. Slavery was a bad thing, cause some white folks didn't treat dere niggers right." She went on. "I was beat just like a man. I got beaten, didn't get no work done. Made my back naked, beat me, wash 'em down with brine. I got scars on my back."

Mary told her she was never beaten, but had seen a man beaten to death. She told the old woman how a man had tried to beat her in Montana and she shot and killed him. Within a short time every black on the train was looking for the black woman who had shot and killed a white man.

When Mary found the old Dunne farm, it was now part of a larger farm and the big house was gone, along with the slave quarters. She tried to find some old friends, but all were gone. She went over to the next farm and found her friend Ella, who sent her tobacco. Ella looked old and poor. Mary stayed with her a couple of days.

Ella wanted to know how Mary got away with carrying her gun around. Mary told her no one challenged her. Ella said she was always scared. "You know, Mary, dey is mighty strict with colored folks, and poor white people too. De Ku Klux come out at night, whipping and hanging people. But dey never bothered me, I too poor."

Mary looked at Ella. "The Kluxes come at me, they speak to my shotgun."

"Mary, I hear you kill a white man trying to whip you?"

"Yes, I killed him with my pistol."

Mary didn't feel at home anymore in Tennessee and felt she shouldn't have come. She tried to find her mother's grave, but all the graves were gone, including Mr. & Mrs. Dunne's. She could not understand how people could plow right over the graves.

It was a long way to travel to stay just a week, but a week was long enough. Mary wanted to leave Tennessee forever. She took the stage back to Nashville and boarded the train in the black cars for the trip to Chicago.

Mary heard that old story again about forty acres and a mule; it made her laugh. They told every ex-slave that, but nobody ever knew anyone who got it. The officers also told them they would get a slave pension. Nothing ever hatched out of that either.

Mary chuckled, "Forty acres and a mule, a parcel of ground to farm." She didn't think she would like to have her forty acres and a mule anywhere in Tennessee. She would rather be back in her room over the saloon in Cascade. But in her heart, she did miss the garden she had had at the mission. Mary said to her eagle, "And I do have you, you dumb old bird."

After Chicago the trains were mixed again, and the farther north and west the train traveled, the more comfortable she felt in her buckskin.

CHAPTER TWENTY-FOUR

A Baby in Marysville

In the late spring of 1896, Mary was able to purchase a small, rundown house in Cascade. The house would keep her busy when she wasn't out on her mail route. The first thing she did was to start her garden and build a small hennery. By the end of summer she had the house and garden in good shape. It wasn't forty acres, but it was her home.

Mary had received word that Mary Gump was pregnant and would have her baby in September. She was hoping to make a surprise run to Marysville, but most trips there were made by the big freight wagons. However, in November, she was offered a few extra dollars to take a freight wagon to Marysville. The driver had quit and supplies needed to be moved. Mary told her employer she would take the freight if she could have a couple of days off in Marysville. She had no way of letting Mary and Joseph know she was coming.

When Mary arrived, she had to ask what house belonged to Joseph Gump. When it was pointed out, Mary thought she should have known it would be the one with the freshest paint and the neatest in every way.

She left the wagon at the freight barn and walked up to the house. When she knocked, Mary came to the door. She let out a scream. "Miss Fields, you're in Marysville! Come in!"

Before Mary could get her buffalo coat off, she was shown the baby, Marguerite. "My, what a beautiful baby you have!"

"Miss Fields, how long are you in Marysville?"

"I get to spend a couple of days."

Everything in the house was perfect; she could see some of the furniture Joseph had made. "Miss Fields, you will stay with us in this room." Again the room was so clean and perfect; it was set up for the baby, but also had a bed for her.

Joseph wouldn't be home until after seven. The two Marys had the afternoon to talk about the mission, since Mary Fields made stops there on her mail run.

When Joseph came in he gave Miss Fields a big hug. "Mary, I miss you and our talks over a glass of whiskey. Would you like one now?"

"I sure would, Joseph, I sure would."

Miss Fields chatted about her job as Mary prepared dinner. Joseph kept Marguerite on his lap. "Joseph, let me hold that child."

At dinner the first thing Joseph asked Mary was whether she had shot any more men. Mary replied, "No, they all run when they hear the name 'Black Mary the Gunfighter.'" Miss Fields started to laugh. "But you remember, Joseph, you the one who taught me how to shoot."

"I know, but you became a much better and faster shot than I am. As they say, you learned too well. I would never go against you."

Miss Fields told Joseph that she could drink in any saloon, because everyone had heard the story about the shooting at the mission and all the saloonkeepers were afraid to throw her out. She made sure she carried a big shotgun wherever she went.

Joseph had to go to work early the next morning, but made Mary promise to meet him at the saloon when he got off work that evening. At quitting time Joseph was waiting at the saloon; when Mary walked in, the place went silent. Joseph went over, took her arm, and walked her up to the bar.

"This is Mary Fields. I want to buy her a whiskey. If anyone objects I will let her kill him."

Everyone started to laugh, and Mary knew they must know the story of Mary Fields. She was the center of attention, with every miner wanting to shake her hand. "Joseph, you got one famous friend, that's the real Black Mary."

"Yes, and she is one tough woman."

That afternoon Mary had gone over to the freight station and gotten her eagle to show Mary Gump, so she had the bird with her at the saloon. One of the miners tried to touch it, and the eagle took a big piece of meat out of his hand. The man let out a scream. All the other men laughed at him. "That's one damn mean bird."

Mary told the man, "You buy him a whiskey, you can pet him."

The miner walked over to the bartender with blood dripping from his hand. "One whiskey for my enemy." He set the drink on the table and all enjoyed the show as the eagle drank his whiskey. Then the miner was able to pet the eagle, and he had to smile.

Dinner was ready when they got back to the house. Joseph got some raw meat, gave it to the eagle, and put the eagle in the barn. Then he told his wife what had happened at the saloon.

Mary Fields told them that she had a house in Cascade, but her address was still "The Saloon, Cascade." The next day was clear and the two Marys took a short walk. All the wives came out to see this woman their husbands were talking about—a woman who could drink in the saloons and had an eagle as a pet.

Mary told of her trip to Tennessee and how poor everyone looked, and how those blacks still weren't treated with any respect. She told how the Ku Klux Klan was putting fear in the people, so that many were afraid to go out at night. The black folks called them "Ku Klux."

"They come right to your house and scare everyone half to death. They take some out and whip them or tie them up by their fingers and toes. One old woman told me they come to her window at night and said, 'Your time ain't long a-coming.' Joseph, the South isn't good for black people. Even my mama's grave is gone."

Joseph told Mary he planned to leave the mines and try to buy a farm near Havre. He wanted to raise pigs and sell the pork to the railroads. She thought he would do well.

When it was time for Miss Fields to leave, Mary and Joseph hated to see her go. Mary loved Miss Fields, who had treated her so well at the mission. She was like a mother in so many ways.

Half the town turned out to see this famous black woman driving a freight wagon in the middle of Montana. Mary waved as she started down the hill with her eagle at her side.

The winter of 1896–97 was cold and the wagons weren't moving. This gave Mary time to work on the inside of her house. In January the temperature fell to 22° below zero, and some days as low as 46° below. On January 28, Cascade was hit by a great blizzard, and the temperature went down to 65° below zero. Mary kept her fire going and only went out to find her chickens.

Reports came in about what had happened to a herd of cattle during this long cold spell. The herd had been driven across the Missouri in early fall to feed on better grass on the northern range. Because little shelter existed on the prairie north of the river, the cattle were half-dead from cold and hunger. Bewildered and blinded by the snow, they had blundered into barbed wire fences and crumpled against them. They were trapped in drifts up to their bellies and stood erect until they froze. Some had fallen into holes in the river ice.

It was impossible to tell how cold it was. A newspaper report described how cowboys dealt with the cold. The cowboys had to don two suits of heavy underwear, two pairs of wool socks, wool pants, two woolen shirts, overalls, leather chaps, wool gloves under leather mittens, heavy blanket-lined overcoats, and fur caps pulled over their ears. Before putting on their socks they would walk in the snow in their bare feet. The chill would cause their feet to warm up. Then they would rub their feet dry, pull on their socks and riding boots, stand in water, and go outside until an airtight sheath of ice would form on their boots. Some wore fur moccasins and overshoes or sheepskin boots.

The cowboys worked to extricate cattle caught in the drifts and tried to herd the dying cattle into ravines for shelter. They also tried to push them away from the treacherous river. The smart cowboys blackened their faces and eyes with lampblack or burnt matches to prevent snow blindness. They wrapped wool cloth with eyeholes cut in it around their faces. They would tie themselves into their saddles, but the icy air cut into their lungs and stomachs; their hands and feet froze. Many of them died and were found tied and frozen to their horses.

There wasn't any way that the mail was going to move until a break in the weather came.

CHAPTER TWENTY-FIVE

Visiting the Mission

Mary was happy to see spring, and as soon as the weather started to warm up and the ground could be worked she had her garden planted.

In June she was making a mail run up to the mission, where she usually spent the night. Joseph had quit his job in Marysville and was on the way to Havre; he was also making a stop at the mission to see his old friends and to give his wife a chance to see Emma and the sisters. They also wanted to show off their baby, Marguerite.

The first to greet them was Miss Fields. You could hear her half a mile away. "Mary, Joseph, let me see that baby again. Been a long time, she sure grown. Oh, how wonderful! Come into the kitchen, still my kitchen, no one big enough 'round here to throw me out when I visit. Coffee, cake, please sit!"

As Mary gave her a big hug, Miss Fields said, "It is so good to see you here at the mission."

"Miss Fields, have you seen Emma yet?"

"Emma is in class but will be out soon."

Joseph told both Marys that he was going to put the horse in the barn and bring in their bags. Miss Fields asked if she could help him. He told her he could do it; she should just stay with Mary.

That evening Joseph and Mary Fields took a walk around the mission. It hadn't changed much in Joseph's eyes, but Mary could see a lot of change. To her mind it was going downhill.

They ran into one of the brothers, who brought them up to date on all the news of the mission. He told them a funny story. In February, a crazy man was running around the mission shooting at random. "Scared, excuse my expression, the hell out of the nuns, bullets whizzing by them when they were coming from Benediction. They all hid in the snow. Father went out to grab the man, but he couldn't find him. Joseph, you should have seen those nuns. Like a covey of quail going all directions. Those were some unhappy nuns."

Joseph and Mary Fields couldn't stop laughing, as it reminded them of seeing the nuns falling on the ice on the way to church. It was easy to picture them diving into the snow as the bullets whizzed past.

Mary remembered that Miss Fields had had a birthday on March 15. She asked her, "Which birthday was this for you?"

"Mary, I was 65 years old this year, I was born in 1832. It sure seems a long time ago."

"Mary," one of the nuns broke in, "you just missed the Feast of Corpus Christi. Emma helped a lot. We had the most beautiful procession. The children made flags and picked flowers. They decorated the whole mission. It was the first big day after the long winter. The little Indian girls strewed flowers during the procession. They were all wearing their pink dresses and white caps, with baskets strung around their necks on pink ribbons. The older Indian girls wore their blue polka-dot dresses. I can remember when Joseph and Miss Fields did the grounds with trees."

Mary Fields smiled. All she could remember was washing, ironing, and storing all those dresses for the next church feast.

"Ah, Mary, here comes Emma now!" One of the nuns pointed to Emma coming from the classroom building. She came bounding into the kitchen.

"That child gets more beautiful every time I see her," Mary Fields said.

Emma hugged her sister, Joseph, and Miss Fields. "It is so good to see all of you here!" She turned to her sister: "Let me see that baby. You know she's my only niece. She is so beautiful! Look at those big black eyes and all that hair. Wait till you see the new bonnet I made her."

At dinner that night it seemed that everyone was talking at once, trying to catch up on the news. After dinner Mary Fields and Joseph slipped off for a shot of Mary's whiskey, a smoke, and a lot of talk. Mary wanted to hear all about Joseph's plans. It felt good for the two of them to be able to sit out in front of Mary's old room and just talk again. Then he told her that he had to turn in. He told her how much he missed her and his old mission jobs, but he was looking forward to having his own farm.

Mary was up early to have coffee with Mary and Joseph, since she had to get back on her mail route. She always hated to say good-bye to them. As usual, there were tears between the two Marys. As Mary Fields drove away, she thought to herself that maybe she should move to Havre, but she had her house and job in Cascade.

The trips to the mission were becoming harder on Mary. Mother Amadeus had been sent to St. Labre's, and it seemed she knew fewer and fewer people at the mission. But her little room or shed was always kept empty for her. It was Mary Fields' room, and only hers.

One time in June 1897, Mary was forced to stay at the mission on account of a terrible lightning and hail storm that beat every plant at the mission right down to the ground. The dams that supplied water to the mission started to overflow and threatened to flood the place.

Mary went out with the brothers to help shore up the dams. They found that a muskrat had made a hole in one of the dams, which they were unable to repair; the roar and rush of the waters could be heard all over the mission and kept everyone awake all night. But the next morning the rains slowed; the dams held and the mission did not flood.

Mary helped the brothers all the next day, but decided to leave when she was told that the bishop would be making a visit on June 28. She told the brothers, "I wanna be long gone before that man gets here."

On a trip in August, Mary was so happy to learn that her friend Mother Amadeus had returned after being absent for eight months. It would make her trips more pleasant.

On October 10, 1898, Mary arrived at the mission just in time to see a new threshing machine harvest over 1,586 bushels of oats from the mission land. The oats were stored in one of the original old mission log cabins.

Mary left the mission the next day. She hadn't traveled far when her horse got scared and went wild, and she was thrown out of her wagon. She was found by a cowboy and taken back to the mission. It was the first time in her life she had to be taken care of instead of taking care of someone else.

She was hurt and badly bruised, but no bones were broken. She would be confined to bed for a week. The cowboy found her wagon, horse, and eagle all in good shape and brought them back to the mission.

Mary still wasn't feeling very well when she left the mission; Mother Amadeus wanted her to stay longer. But Mary felt that she had to get the wagon back to Cascade. When she got there, everyone thought she had been in a fight with a wildcat, with all the bruises and cuts on her arms and face; she still wasn't walking very well.

In December, a huge bell weighing 860 pounds arrived in Cascade to be taken to the mission. It was a present from Father Sandavet. The mission wanted the bell delivered so they could usher in the New Year, 1899.

A special wagon had to be rigged to haul this big bell up to the mission, and since Mary knew the trail best, she made the delivery. The bell was hung by the brothers, and it did indeed usher in the New Year. Everyone at the mission got a turn at ringing the bell.

Mary stayed for two weeks so she could celebrate the anniversary of Mother Amadeus' arrival at the mission fifteen years earlier, on January 15. Mary had also been in Montana for fifteen years.

When Mary returned to Cascade, terrible winds and snowstorms started, making it impossible for her to deliver mail or any supplies to the mission. She was pleased that by the end of February she was able to make her regular mail deliveries and trips to the mission again.

On June 26, the bishop was going to St. Peter's for the closing of the school year. On his way he made a stop in Cascade for a meeting with the Episcopal bishop, Reverend H. Arts. As the

Reverend Arts was passing the saloon, he was thrown from his buggy and the buggy's wheels ran over him.

Mary stood in the window of the saloon laughing: here was this Catholic Bishop Brondel dragging this Episcopal Bishop Arts out of the street. Both their fancy suits were dirty.

The saloonkeeper came over. "Mary, did you smack or spook that bishop's horse?"

"I wish to God I had."

The Episcopal bishop wasn't hurt, but it was going to take a long time to get that horse and buggy back. Mary could see them both leaving Cascade at a fast pace. And she wasn't about to help chase them down.

Early that fall, Mary decided to make a trip up to Havre to see the Gumps. She had already received the news that Mary was expecting again, and the baby would be there by the time she made the trip. The trip was easy since she knew the way, and she had no trouble finding their home. When she arrived, she was greeted by Mary, Joseph, Emma, Marguerite, and little Leo.

The house was beautiful: it had a big kitchen, which Mary noticed first, a living room, a parlor, and four bedrooms. Mary was taken to her room. As in the rest of the house, everything was perfect, and she could see many things Joseph had made.

After dinner the first night, which Mary helped to prepare, she and Joseph sat out on the porch and had a drink and a smoke. Joseph told her all about his pig farm and how he was selling all his pork, hams, and bacon to the railroad and hotels; he couldn't keep up with the demand. His only real problem was his wife's health: she still had problems with her lungs. Mary Fields had always worried about Mary.

She told Joseph about the mission and all the changes that were going on, and about the talk of moving the mission to Great Falls. She told Joseph she was making more money from her eggs, chickens, and vegetable garden than from her job. She also told him about her fall from the wagon. At her age she was having trouble recovering and was thinking more and more about retiring. Joseph told her she would always be welcome in Havre.

Mary spent four happy days with Mary, Joseph, and their family. She was able to help Mary in the house and Joseph with the smoking of his pork. She told him his smoked meat was the best she had ever eaten. Joseph told her it was smoked the way he had learned from the German brothers at the mission. When she left, he wrapped a couple of hams for her to take back to Cascade with her. She told him she would serve them to her guests for dinner.

As usual, it was hard for both Marys to say good-bye. Mary Fields told Mary to take care of herself and keep writing. They had shared a lot together.

In early fall of 1900, Mary Fields was at the mission and Mother Amadeus was telling her about her new experiment in the education of the Indians. She had had seven Cheyenne girls and eight boys sent to her from St. Labre's. This new life away from their environment would help the children to adjust to future changes. Each year, they would return to their families for a vacation. The boys would be given a horse for their use and care.

Mary could feel herself becoming angry. It was 1900 and they were still taking children from their families so they could adjust to the white man's ways.

In January 1901, Mary received a letter from Mary Gump telling her that she had caught a cold that went into pneumonia again. She had become very sick, and the doctor warned her she must be careful in the future with her health. With Emma's help with the children, she was able to take better care of herself. Mary Fields made a promise to herself that she would make a trip up to Havre in the spring.

Chapter Twenty-Six

Mary's Last Years

Mary Fields quit her mail route job in the spring of 1901. She was now sixty-nine years old and feeling her age. Her old friend the eagle had died that winter. This was a real loss; no matter how much she said she hated that bird, she did love it.

Mary had her garden and chickens and was taking in washing. She also ran an eating house, which was the best in the area.

Father Eberschweiler had the Gump family at his church in Havre. He would always stop at Mary's house on his way to Helena to keep her informed about them—and to get a good meal. He would always remind her how she had been injured in October 1878 and how she had become repentant and returned to her religious duties. She had sat in the front pew in a blue challis dress that was made by one of the sisters, who labored all night to make that dress for her. "Mary," he said, "you returned to God."

"Father, every time you come here you tell me that story. That was the last time I wore a dress, and I told you God and me understand each other. I tell you my church is in my heart."

"Mary, you are closer to God than anyone I know." Father Eberschweiler gave Mary a big hug. "And you are a darned good cook."

"Father, you like all men, get to them through their stomachs."

In July of 1902, Mary Fields got a letter from Mary Gump saying that Joseph had sold their farm and butcher shop and they were moving out to Spokane, Washington, where Joseph's mother lived. She would write as soon as they were settled.

In October 1902, Mother Amadeus was on a train a few miles from Billings, Montana, when the train was wrecked and Mother Amadeus was severely injured. She was taken first to St. Vincent's Hospital in Billings; then on November 4 she was moved to Helena, where her impacted fracture of the femur could be treated. She would be under the care of a friend of the sisters, Dr. Treacy.

Mary Fields went to Helena to see her friend, who wasn't responding to treatment. Dr. Treacy was worried about Mother Amadeus's knee becoming stiff and advised her to go to California for rest and treatment. On April 3, 1903, Mary was there to say good-bye to Mother Amadeus as she left for California.

On November 3, 1903, Bishop Brondel died. The papers read, "The great missionary, Bishop Brondel, has died." Mary had a drink in his memory. She could hear Mother Amadeus: "The saintly bishop had been the devoted friend of the Ursulines from the first day they arrived in Miles City in 1884."

In March 1904, Mother Amadeus returned to Montana, called there by the serious illness of one of the sisters at St. Paul's Mission on the Fort Belknap Reservation. While there she herself developed pneumonia and was close to death. Dr. Irwin came from Great Falls and Mary Fields from Cascade to attend to her.

The two women spent many hours talking about the years they had spent together. They were both seventy-two years old. After her recovery, Mother Amadeus spent the remainder of her stay visiting the Montana missions, while Mary Fields returned to her cottage business in Cascade.

Mary enjoyed the letters she received from the Gumps. Mary's health was better. Joseph was working as a fireman in Spokane, and the children were doing well. The letters always ended by asking Mary to come out to Spokane to visit them, but Mary knew she would never leave Montana again.

In January 1908, fire destroyed the boys' house and the Indian girls' dorm at St. Peter's Mission. The boys' school was closed and the pupils sent home.

January 18, 1909, marked the twenty-fifth anniversary of the arrival of the Ursulines in Montana. A celebration was held in Miles City and Mary Fields was invited to attend. She stayed at the convent with the sisters; she was always a novelty for the young sisters to see. Mary Fields was a legend among the Ursulines. She would make a trip once a year out to St. Peter's as she watched it slowly disappear.

Starting in 1910, full plans were being made to move the academy to Great Falls. The Ursulines felt St. Peter's was not easy of access, and they wanted to attract day pupils as well as boarding students. Mother Amadeus again asked Mary to come to Great Falls and help with the new school, but Mary said she was too old and wanted to stay in Cascade.

Mary Fields, or Black Mary, was famous all over Montana. Great Falls was the home of a young cowboy artist named Charlie Russell. In a pen-and-ink sketch called "A Quiet Day in Cascade," he immortalized Mary Fields. Depicting her as being upset by a mule kicking over her basket of eggs, Russell also wove into the picture events in the history of Cascade. The picture was given to the Ursulines.

Mary became very ill in 1914 and was taken to Columbus Hospital in Great Falls, where she died. She was buried in a small cemetery outside of Cascade on the road that leads to St. Peter's Mission.

Her headstone is a large boulder with just the words:

Mary Fields
1832 – 1914

Epilogue

On my last visit to St. Peter's Mission, very little remained. A large pile of stone marks the site of the convent, school and dormitory. The little log church still stands, as it did when it was built in 1878. They still say Mass there every Christmas Eve, and the small church fills with people who come from all over the area. The "Opera House" is still standing, but has become a cattle barn. The boys' school closed in 1896 and burned to the ground in 1908.

The most extensive destruction of the mission came about on the morning of November 12, 1918, when the large stone convent, school and dormitory burned to the ground as well. When this building burned there were still seven sisters and forty-two children living in it. The mission was then closed and moved to Great Falls, Montana.

The small cemetery where my grandmother's brother Lee Roy is buried still remains on a small hill overlooking the mission site. The cemetery is fenced and still used by local families.

Mary Fields worked hard in the development of St. Peter's Mission, but, perhaps fortunately, she did not live to see its end.

Bibliography

Banks, Eleanor. *Wandersong.* Caxton Printers, 1950.

Burlingame, Merrill G. *The Montana Frontier.* Big Sky Books, 1980.

Cody, William F. and Henry Inman. *The Great Salt Lake Trail.* Macmillan, 1898.

Cooper, John M. *The Gros Ventres of Montana: Part II, Religion and Ritual.* The Catholic University of America Press, 1975.

Costello, Gladys. "White Man Left His Name to a Mountain." *Phillips County News,* 1987.

"Death of James Wells." *The River Press,* Fort Benton, February 11, 1885.

Dixon, Dr. Joseph K. *The Vanishing Race—The Last Great Indian Council.*

Douglas, Frederick. *My Bondage and My Freedom.* Dover Publications, Inc., 1969.

Flannery, Regina. *The Gros Ventres of Montana: Part I, Social Life.* The Catholic University of America Press, 1975.

Fort Belknap Education Department. *Recollections of Fort Belknap's Past.* Fort Belknap Indian Community, 1982.

Fort Belknap Education Department. *War Stories of the White Clay People.* Fort Belknap Indian Community, 1982.

Fowler, Loretta. *Shared Symbols, Contested Meanings: Gros Ventre Culture and History, 1778–1984.* Cornell University Press, 1987.

Hardin, Floyd. *Campfires and Cowchips.* Floyd Hardin, 1972.

"Historic Bulding." *The River Press,* Fort Benton, December 13, 1989.

Horse Capture, George, editor. *The Seven Visions of Bull Lodge.* University of Nebraska Press, 1992.

Howard, Joseph Kinsey. *Montana: High, Wide, and Handsome.* University of Nebraska Press, 1983.

Jackson, W. Turrentine. *Wells Fargo Stagecoaching in Montana Territory.* Montana Historical Society Press, 1979.

Jacobs, Harriet A. *Life of a Slave Girl.* Harvard University Press, 1987.

Kroeber, A. L. *Ethnology of the Gros Ventres.* American Museum of Natural History, Anthropological Paper, vol. 1 part 4, 1908.

Lavender, David. *Let Me Be Free.* Harper Collins, 1992.

MacDonald, Henry. "A Pioneer." *The River Press,* Fort Benton, January 26, 1887.

Marshall, S. L. A. *Crimsoned Prairie: The Indian Wars.* Da Capo Press, 1972.

McBride, Genevieve. *The Bird Tail.* Vantage Press, 1974.

McHugh, Tom. *The Time of the Buffalo.* University of Nebraska Press, 1979.

Morgan, L. H. *The Indian Journal, 1859–1982.* University of Michigan Press, 1959.

Northup, Solomon. *Twelve Years a Slave.* Dover Publications, Inc., 1970.

Noyes, A. J. *In the Land of Chinook: The Story of Blaine County.* State Publishing Co., 1917.

Overholser, Joel. *Fort Benton: World's Innermost Port.* River Press, 1987.

Overholser, Joel. "James Wells Had Very Busy, Adventurous Life in Area." *The River Press,* Fort Benton, August 19, 1981.

Palladino, Laurence Benedict. *Indian & White in the Northwest: A History of Catholicity in Montana.* J. Murphy & Co., 1894.

Schoenberg, Wilfred. *Jesuits in Montana.* The Oregon Jesuit, 1960.

Stannard, David E. *American Holocaust.* Oxford University Press, 1992.

Toole, K. Ross. *Montana: An Uncommon Land.* University of Oklahoma Press, 1943.

Utley, Robert M. *The Indian Frontier of the American West, 1846–1890.* University of New Mexico Press, 1987.

Vogel, Virgil J. *American Indian Medicine.* University of Oklahoma Press, 1990.

Washburn, Wilcomb E. *Red Man's Land/White Man's Law.* University of Oklahoma Press, 1995.

White, Jon Manchip. *Everyday Life of the North American Indians.* Dorset Press, 1979.

Willard, John. *Adventure Trails in Montana.* State Publishing Co., 1964.

Winther, Oscar Osburn. *Via Western Express & Stagecoach.* Stanford University Press, 1945.

Yetman, Norman R. *Voices from Slavery.* Dover Publications, Inc., 1970.

UNPUBLISHED SOURCES

Bureau of Indian Affairs, Fort Belknap Reservation: Office files.

Montana Historical Society, Helena: Papers of T. C. Power.

National Archives, Records of the Bureau of Indian Affairs, Washington, D.C.: Central files, Fort Belknap Agency. Indian Census Rolls, 1888–1911.

More Fascinating Books from Wild Goose Press

James Wells of Montana: The Years 1860–1885
BY JAMES A. FRANKS
261 pp. Paper. ISBN 0-9657173-0-5. $14.95

The history of the West is revealed in the accomplishments of James Wells (1840–1885). James A. Franks describes the life of this Pony Express rider, stagecoach driver and fur trapper who married a Gros Ventre Indian woman and became immersed in the customs of her tribe. Running trading posts, making a cattle drive from Texas, founding an important ranch on the Judith River, Wells had great insight into the future of Montana, though he could not have predicted the unjust treatment his Indian wife and children would receive after his death.

"An immensely readable and fascinating book, written with rare humor and warmth . . . James Wells of Montana *is a serious moral vision of the American West and the passing of the Indian way of life."*
—DONALD J. YOUNG, author of *The Reunion* and *The Lion's Share*

"Bury My Heart at Wounded Knee *was the big picture* . . . James Wells of Montana *is the personal story that says it all."*
—JAMES R. COX, author of *Classics in the Literature of Mountaineering*

Mary Wells
BY JAMES A. FRANKS
213 pp. Paper. ISBN 0-9657173-3-X. $12.95.

Mary Wells is the second in a series of historical biographies by James A. Franks, the subject's grandson. Mary Wells is the intriguing matriarch of a pioneer family torn apart by a cultural clash between the Plains Indians and the white civilization to which the Wells belonged. As stated by Diana Wyatt, Montana State Representative, "James A. Franks writes from the heart, with historical acumen . . ." about this family's struggles in Montana through the late 1800s. This is a story guaranteed to draw you in.

Grandma Franks' Cookbook
COMPILED BY JAMES A. FRANKS
332 pp. Paper. ISBN 0-9657173-1-3. $24.95.

A delicious, historical treasure full of authentic recipes from the turn of the century. Ida Franks' love of cooking shines through this book with over 1500 recipes, including the collection of the Jolly Thimble Club circa 1907. Pages of cakes, whole chapters of pies, putting food by, helpful hints, hot toddies, and how to not only serve tea but divine with tea leaves. Breads, muffins, meats and vegetables all taste good from this collection of recipes. This fine treasure is lovingly compiled by grandson and historian James A. Franks.

Miss Leslie's Secrets: What Every Bride Should Know
BY ELIZA LESLIE
520 pp. Hardcover. ISBN 0-96571732-1. $18.95

Was it really so different in 1854? Rediscover the adventures of domestic life in Miss Leslie's classic guide to cooking and housekeeping. Originally published in 1854 by Eliza Leslie, this reproduced book contains 1,011 recipes that will happily feed families for generations; a treasure for any bride. A fascinating journal filled with seasonal menus, oils, home remedies and perfumery. Recipes range from rhubarb cups, onion custard and fried cabbage to venison, fresh trout and dressing terrapins.

"All the recipes in this book are new, and have been fully tried and tested by the author, and none of them whatever are contained in any other work but this. In it there will be found one thousand and eleven new recipes, all useful, some ornamental, and all invaluable to every miss or family in the world. In it will also be found popular and useful suggestions of immense value in every household, adding greatly to its convenience, its comfort and economy. No woman ought to be without this book."
—LADIES NATIONAL MAGAZINE, 1854

To order any of the above titles, contact:

Wild Goose Press
719 Fairmount Avenue
Santa Cruz, CA 95062
E-mail: Wldgoose2@aol.com
Phone: 831-426-6850
Fax: 831-426-6850